LIVING IN THE WILD: SEA MAMMALS

ORCAS

Claire Throp

Raintree

Raintree is an imprint of Capstone Global Library Limited, a company incorporated in England and Wales having its registered office at 7 Pilgrim Street, London, EC4V 6LB – Registered company number: 6695582

www.raintreepublishers.co.uk
myorders@raintreepublishers.co.uk

Text © Capstone Global Library Limited 2013
First published in hardback in 2013
First published in paperback in 2014
The moral rights of the proprietor have been asserted.

Edited by Adam Miller, Andrew Farrow, and Laura Knowles
Designed by Steve Mead
Picture research by Mica Brančić
Original illustrations © Capstone Global Library Ltd 2013
Illustrations by HL Studios
Originated by Capstone Global Library Ltd
Printed and bound in China by CTPS

ISBN 978 1 406 25010 7 (hardback)
16 15 14 13 12
10 9 8 7 6 5 4 3 2 1

ISBN 978 1 406 25017 6 (paperback)
17 16 15 14
10 9 8 7 6 5 4 3 2 1

British Library Cataloguing in Publication Data
Throp, Claire.
 Orcas. -- (Living in the wild. Sea Mammals)
599.5'36-dc23
A full catalogue record for this book is available from the British Library.

Acknowledgements
We would like to thank the following for permission to reproduce photographs: Alamy pp. 4 (© Danita Delimont Creative), 17 (© nrmarinelife), 25 (© Brandon Cole Marine Photography), 7 (© Streeter Photography); Corbis p. 22 (Minden Pictures/© Tui De Roy); FLPA pp. 13 (Minden Pictures/Norbert Wu), 26 (Minden Pictures/© Flip Nicklin), 36 (Minden Pictures/© Flip Nicklin); Getty Images p. 11 (Discovery Channel Images/Jeff Foott), 15 (All Canada Photos/Rolf Hicker), 23 (Oxford Scientific/Gerard Soury), 29 (Photographer's Choice/Johnny Johnson), 45 (Dorling Kindersley); Nature Picture Library pp. 10 (© Todd Pusser), 16 (© Wild Wonders of Europe/Aukan), 21 (© Mark Carwardine), 27 (© Brandon Cole), 30 (© Brandon Cole), 33 (© Solvin Zankl), 34 (© Kathryn Jeffs), 39 (© Brandon Cole), 40 (© Todd Pusser); New Zealand Herald p. 38 (APN Images); Photoshot pp. 31 (Norbert Wu), 35 (Francois Gohie), 43 (Juniors Tierbildarchiv); Shutterstock pp. 6 (© lantapix), 19 (© Manamana), 32 (© Minden Pictures), 41 (© Minden Pictures).

Cover photograph of an adult orca with an open mouth reproduced with permission of Superstock/© Gerard Lacz.

Every effort has been made to contact copyright holders of any material reproduced in this book. Any omissions will be rectified in subsequent printings if notice is given to the publisher.

Disclaimer
All the internet addresses (URLs) given in this book were valid at the time of going to press. However, due to the dynamic nature of the internet, some addresses may have changed, or sites may have changed or ceased to exist since publication. While the author and publisher regret any inconvenience this may cause readers, no responsibility for any such changes can be accepted by either the author or the publisher.

Contents

Some words are shown in bold, **like this**. You can find out what they mean by looking in the glossary.

What are sea mammals?

What's that huge, dark shape moving through the water? Suddenly, an orca leaps out of the sea, twists round, and splashes back into the water.

An orca, or killer whale, might look like a large fish but it is a sea **mammal**. Mammals have a backbone, fur or hair on their bodies, and use lungs to breathe. They give birth to live young and mothers feed their babies milk. Does this description sound familiar? It should – humans are also mammals.

Sea mammals live and feed in the sea. There are four groups: whales and dolphins; seals, sea lions, and walruses; manatees and dugongs; and sea otters and polar bears. They are all excellent swimmers and divers. They are also known as **marine** mammals. Marine means "of the sea".

These sea lions watch carefully as orcas swim in the shallow water. Orcas are predators that hunt sea lions.

Meet the sea mammals

There are around 130 different types, or **species**, of sea mammal. They have adapted in different ways to live in the sea:

Type of sea mammal	How do they move?	Where do they live?
Whales and dolphins	use tail, fins, and flippers	These sea mammals live in water all the time.
Manatees and dugongs	use tail and flippers	
Seals, sea lions, and walruses	use flippers	These sea mammals spend some of their time in water, and some on land.
Sea otters	use legs and tail	
Polar bears	use legs	

Cetaceans

Whales and dolphins are **cetaceans**. There are about 90 species of cetaceans, divided into two groups: toothed cetaceans, such as the orca, and baleen cetaceans, such as the blue whale. Cetaceans have very little hair on their body but do have a thick layer of **blubber** to keep them warm. They come to the surface to breathe through a blowhole. Toothed cetaceans have one blowhole and baleen cetaceans have two. Toothed cetaceans use **echolocation** to find prey but baleens do not. Instead of teeth, baleen cetaceans have plates in their top jaw, through which they sieve small prey such as **plankton**.

SIZE DIFFERENCE

Orcas may look huge but they are not very big in comparison to the largest sea mammal, the blue whale. The largest blue whale ever measured was 33.5 metres (110 feet). The biggest ever orca measured only 9.8 metres (32 feet).

What are orcas?

Orcas are the largest members of the dolphin family. Males can grow to lengths of 9 metres (30 feet) and weigh up to 9 tonnes. Females are smaller but can still measure up to 8 metres (26 feet) and weigh up to 8 tonnes. They can reach swimming speeds of up to 55 kilometres per hour (34 miles per hour). However, they usually swim at 5 to 6 kilometres per hour (3 to 4 miles per hour).

Features of orcas

Orcas have large black and white torpedo-shaped bodies that help them to swim fast. They have a strong tail, pectoral fins to help them steer, and a dorsal fin that helps them to balance. A thick layer of blubber helps them to float and stay warm. Their jaws are powerful and they usually swallow prey whole.

Here you can see the size of an orca compared to a human.

Orcas are **social** animals and mainly travel in groups, called **pods**, of up to 40 orcas. They are very good at working together particularly when hunting.

DR MICHAEL BIGG

Dr Michael Bigg (born 1939) discovered a new way of researching orcas in 1972, using photo identification. He realized that orcas can be recognized in photos by their dorsal fin or saddle patch, which are different for every orca. Scientists can now count rather than guess the number of orcas in a particular area and study the lives of individual orcas.

Females and young orcas have small, curved dorsal fins. Males have much taller, triangular-shaped dorsal fins, which can reach 1.8 metres (nearly 6 feet) in height.

How are orcas classified?

Classification is the way that scientists group living things together according to the characteristics that they share. This allows us to identify living things and help us understand why they live where they do and behave the way they do.

Classification groups

In classification, animals are split into various groups. The standard groups are Kingdom, Phylum, Class, Order, Family, Genus, and Species. Animals are given an internationally recognized two-part Latin name. This helps to avoid confusion if animals are known by different common names in different countries. The orca's Latin name is *Orcinus orca*, for example.

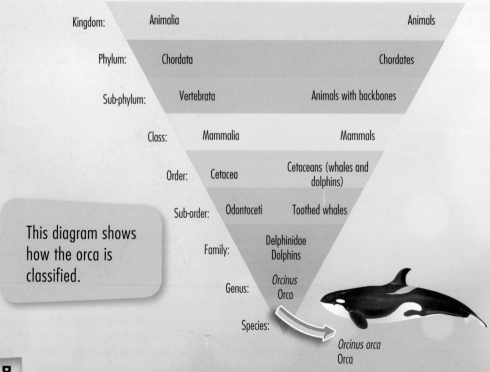

Kingdom:	Animalia	Animals
Phylum:	Chordata	Chordates
Sub-phylum:	Vertebrata	Animals with backbones
Class:	Mammalia	Mammals
Order:	Cetacea	Cetaceans (whales and dolphins)
Sub-order:	Odontoceti	Toothed whales
Family:	Delphinidae	Dolphins
Genus:	*Orcinus* Orca	
Species:	*Orcinus orca* Orca	

This diagram shows how the orca is classified.

Early orcas

At first, mammals only lived on land but around 55 million years ago some moved to the sea – no one knows why. The earliest known orca-like creature was *O. citonensis*, which lived about 2.6 to 5.3 million years ago. It was smaller than the modern orca and was more like a dolphin. Orcas are now classified as *Odontoceti* or toothed whales, of which there are 71 species.

WHEN IS AN ORCA LIKE A HIPPOPOTAMUS?

Until recently scientists thought that cetaceans were descended from hoofed mammals such as cows and horses. Now they think it is more likely that cetaceans such as the orca are distantly related to hippopotamuses! They both have fatty areas in their heads that can give off sounds. They can hear through their lower jaws and there is a close blood match.

This family tree shows some of the whale's distant ancestors.

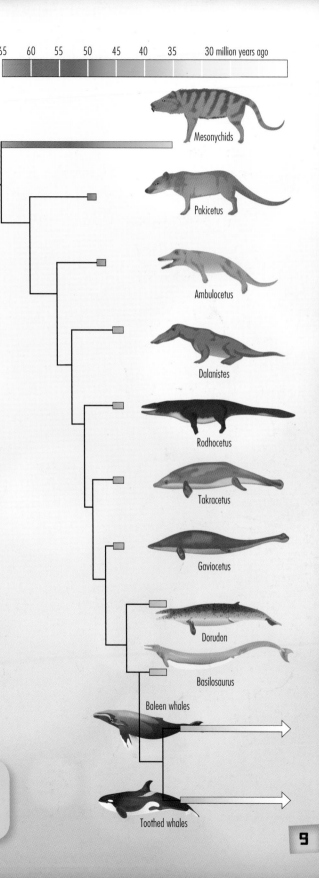

65   60   55   50   45   40   35   30 million years ago

Mesonychids

Pakicetus

Ambulocetus

Dalanistes

Rodhocetus

Takracetus

Gaviocetus

Dorudon

Basilosaurus

Baleen whales

Toothed whales

Types of orca

Orcas living in the Pacific Ocean are well studied and there are three types. **Residents** spend most of their lives in one area. They usually eat fish, such as salmon and herring. **Transients** don't stay in one place for very long. They move around in smaller pods than residents. They travel further for food and eat other sea mammals, such as seals and sea birds. Offshore orcas are the third type, although not as much is known about them because they do not come close to shore very often. They are thought to live in large pods.

Transient orcas, such as these ones, make much less noise than resident orcas.

There is still much to learn about orcas.

How many species?

For a long time scientists have thought that orcas belong to only one species, *Orcinus orca*. But now some scientists are beginning to think that transient and offshore orcas are separate sub-species because they do not seem to mate or mix with the residents. There is a noticeable difference in diet, behaviour, and the shape of their dorsal fin. Orcas in Antarctica have also been divided into three groups depending on their size and diet: Types A, B, and C. Scientists are still not sure whether there are separate species of orca but research continues.

Scientists also believe that orcas are becoming two species in the North Atlantic Ocean around the United Kingdom. Researchers think the orcas can be divided into two groups based on their size, diet, and where they travel. There are a number of obvious differences including the fact that male Type 2 orcas are nearly 2 metres (6 ½ feet) longer than Type 1 males – a big difference!

Where do orcas live?

A **habitat** is the place where an animal lives. The habitat has to provide everything the animal needs from food to shelter. An animal is dependent on its habitat.

Orcas can be found in all the oceans of the world, but usually only in small populations. Orcas have been spotted in tropical waters around Hawaii and Australia, but are more common in colder oceans. Orcas can be seen regularly in the seas around Scotland, Iceland, and Norway. They often swim into areas of thick ice in search of prey in Alaska and Antarctica.

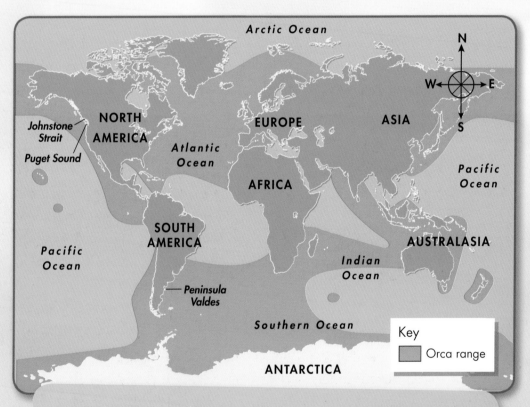

This map shows the main areas where orcas can be found. Some orcas stay in certain areas, such as the southern resident orcas that live in the Puget Sound in the Pacific Ocean.

Offshore orcas have not been well studied but they seem to prefer deep ocean. Most other orcas like coastal waters. They are mainly seen no more than 800 kilometres (500 miles) from the shore where the water is no more than 200 metres (656 feet) deep.

Some oceans are more difficult to live in than others. Orcas living in Antarctica might need to break through ice to breathe.

Migration

Orcas are known to **migrate** long distances in search of their prey. The northeastern Atlantic orcas follow herring, for example. While little is known about offshore orcas, they have been recorded travelling thousands of kilometres in one direction. The movements of orcas can also be affected seasonally by the melting and freezing of pack ice in some oceans.

What adaptations help orcas survive?

An **adaptation** is something that allows an animal to live in a particular place in a particular way. Animals develop adaptations as species evolve over thousands of years.

Body shape

Moving on land is easy because there is little **resistance** from air but moving forward in water is much harder. So orcas have adapted by streamlining their bodies as much as possible. Orcas have torpedo-shaped bodies with a layer of blubber and very little fur or hair.

An orca's tail helps it to move through the sea. The tail has two flat paddles called flukes (see photo). The **horizontal** flukes move up and down to push the orca along. This is different to fish that move their **vertical** tails from side-to-side in order to swim forwards.

The dorsal fin is used partly to help with balance in the water but it has another use: controlling body temperature. When an orca is swimming hard and gets hot, extra heat can escape through the dorsal fin. Some heat also escapes through the tail and pectoral fin.

SKIN GROWTH

An orca's skin grows 290 times faster than that on a human arm!

Blubber

Bodies lose heat around 25 times faster in water than on land. To cope with this, orcas have a layer of blubber on their bodies. The blubber is 7 to 10 centimetres (3 to 4 inches) thick. The blubber is used not only to keep orcas warm but also as a store of food and to help them float in water.

There are no bones in the flukes. This means that some large males have flukes that curve at the edges.

Colouring

The colouring of orcas' bodies helps them to hide. Their bodies are light underneath, so prey looking up from below find it hard to see the orca. They are dark on top so they are less easily seen from above. The pattern also helps to disguise the orca because it breaks up the huge size of the animal. Prey might not feel so threatened because they don't realize its size – until it's too late!

Resident and transient orcas have different diving habits. Transients usually stay under water for longer periods.

Breathing and diving

Orcas have to come to the surface to breathe. The orca has a blowhole (like a person's nostrils) on top of its head so it can take a breath straightaway. When it breathes out, the air is pushed out so quickly that a spray of water shoots into the air. This is called blowing or spouting. The orca closes its blowhole while it is diving under water.

Orcas can dive to depths of at least 100 metres (328 feet). Like other cetaceans, orcas can dive for quite long periods. They can slow their heartbeat from 60 to 30 beats a minute. They save oxygen by pushing it towards the parts of their body that need it most – the heart, lungs, and brain. Orcas can hold their breath for up to 12 minutes but usually their dives do not last more than a few minutes.

Jaws and teeth

Orcas don't chew their food. Their mouths have been adapted for ripping and tearing prey instead. They have large jaws with strong muscles and 40 to 56 teeth. They rip off chunks of prey or swallow it whole.

An orca's teeth measure nearly 8 centimetres (3 inches) long.

Echolocation

It can be difficult to see prey in dark, murky oceans. Orcas have developed a system of echolocation to help them find prey and build up a picture of their surroundings. They make a series of clicks that pass through a fatty part of their forehead called the melon. This focuses the sound into two beams in front of them. The sound bounces off nearby objects and back to the orca. The orca feels the bounces, or echoes, through its lower jaw, which also has a fatty area that joins up with the orca's ear. The echoes tell the orca about the size, shape, and travelling speed of an object as well as other information about its surroundings. **Sonar**, a communication method used by the navy, can confuse sea mammals because it sounds very similar to echolocation.

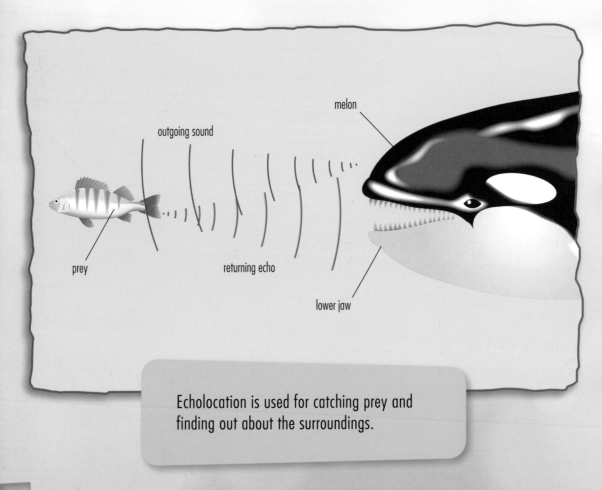

melon

outgoing sound

prey

returning echo

lower jaw

Echolocation is used for catching prey and finding out about the surroundings.

Noise from ships' engines can interfere with orcas' echolocation.

Orcas that eat fish tend to use echolocation more than those that feed on other sea mammals. This is because mammals can hear the clicks made by orcas while most fish cannot. It is possible that sea mammals may have time to escape.

CLICK TRAIN

The series of clicks that orcas make during echolocation are called click trains.

Senses

Orcas have good eyesight both in and out of the water but no sense of smell. As air-breathers that spend most of their time under water, orcas would not be able to use smell effectively. Their hearing is much better than that of humans and they receive many sounds through their lower jaw.

What do orcas eat?

Living things in any habitat depend on each other. This is called **interdependence**. Animals eat other animals or plants in order to get energy. They in turn may be eaten by bigger animals. These links between animals and plants are called **food chains**. Many connected food chains add up to make a **food web**. The more connections there are in a food web, the less it will be affected if one organism dies out.

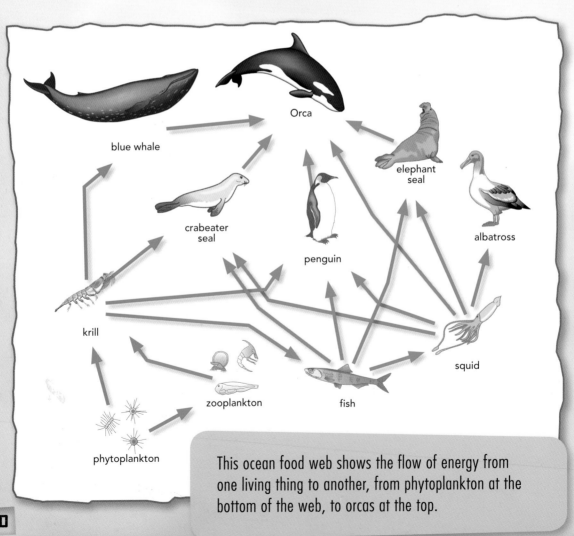

blue whale

Orca

crabeater seal

penguin

elephant seal

albatross

krill

squid

zooplankton

fish

phytoplankton

This ocean food web shows the flow of energy from one living thing to another, from phytoplankton at the bottom of the web, to orcas at the top.

A food chain starts with a plant because plants are the only organisms that can make their own food. They are called producers. In an ocean food web, the producers are plant-like organisms, called phytoplankton, and plants, such as sea grasses. Animals are consumers because they consume, or eat, other animals. Orcas are called carnivores because they eat meat. Animals that eat other animals are known as predators. The animals they eat are known as prey. The orca is the top predator in the sea.

An orca that has successfully caught a herring finds that it attracts a lot of attention!

Finding food

Orcas hunt for food in the water and sometimes on ice or the shore. They have different ways of catching prey, many of which involve teamwork. A pod can chase a minke whale or Dall's porpoise for hours by hunting as a team. One orca chases the prey and then another takes over until the prey is exhausted and can be eaten. Sometimes, however, orcas just follow fishermen and suck the fish off the line leaving only the mouths of the fish behind!

Different diets

Different types of orcas have different diets. Residents eat fish and squid while transients eat sea mammals, such as seals and other whales. The diet of offshore orcas is not known for certain but it is thought that they sometimes feast on sharks. In the northeast Pacific, researchers have seen orcas catch and eat 16 Pacific sleeper sharks in just two feeding sessions.

Playing with food

It is not just human children that play with their food – orcas do, too! Orcas in Argentina come right up to the shore to catch baby sea lions. However, the orca may not eat the sea lion straightaway. The orca flicks the animal up in the air with its tail a few times for fun before finally swallowing it whole.

The diet of some orcas includes fish called stingrays, which they hold on to by the tail.

Sea lion pups are easier to catch than adults.

Sharing food

In the waters around New Zealand, adult male orcas sometimes share their catches with their calves. They catch manta rays, a type of fish, and flip them onto their backs. This causes the fish to relax and not try to escape. The male then passes the ray to his calf or another orca, which then kills the fish. The two share the meal. Orcas living near Norway eat herring. They stun the fish with tail slaps before feeding. They and other orcas then eat the stunned herring.

HOW MUCH DO ORCAS EAT?

Orcas eat 3 to 4 per cent of their body weight in food a day. While it is still growing, a calf needs to eat 10 per cent of its body weight in a day.

What is an orca's life cycle?

The life cycle of an animal covers its birth to its death and all the different stages in between. Sea mammals go through three main stages: birth, youth, and adulthood. Adulthood is when they reproduce and have young themselves.

MEASURING AGE

Scientists have discovered that it is possible to measure the age of orcas by counting growth rings in their teeth, much as we do with growth rings in trees.

Mating

Not much is known about the mating habits of wild orcas. Scientists have mainly studied **captive** orcas. Orcas can mate at any time of year, although some orca populations give birth at particular times of the year. Orcas in the northeast Pacific Ocean, for example, often give birth from October to March.

Orcas do not choose a partner for life. They can have many partners over their lifetimes. In the northeast Pacific, many resident pods join together into a superpod and then socializing and mating takes place.

Orca calves suckle for only 5 to 10 seconds at a time to start with but they do this several times an hour.

Pregnancy and birth

Pregnancy lasts 15 to 18 months before the mother gives birth to one calf in the water, usually tail first. This is so it doesn't drown. The mother pushes the baby up to the surface quickly so that it can take a breath. When a calf is born it is already 2.6 metres (8 ½ feet) long and weighs about 180 kilograms (395 pounds). When it is first born, an orca's dorsal fin and tail flukes are soft and bendy. They gradually stiffen as the orca gets older.

Orca calves **suckle** for at least a year. Their mother's milk has a lot of fat in it to help the calves quickly build up the layer of blubber on their bodies.

Young orcas

Mothers stay close to their calves to protect them. Calves swim in their mother's slipstream, a current of water made as the mother swims. The calf uses less energy when it swims in the slipstream, and this helps it to keep up with the rest of the pod.

Calves remain dependent on their mothers for up to 10 years but most are **weaned** between one and two years of age. Mothers teach their calves how and where to hunt.

Young orcas have plenty of energy for leaping out of the water!

Male orcas help to protect the pod, but have no involvement in looking after their own calves.

The cycle begins again...

Females can become pregnant when they reach the age of 6 to 10 years. Males have to wait till they are big enough to be able to compete with other males. This is usually when they reach about 6 metres (20 feet), around the age of 13. Female orcas give birth every three to five years for around 25 years. When they can no longer have young, the females help out younger mothers with babysitting and teaching young orcas how to hunt.

Orcas have a long lifespan in the wild, particularly females. One female was known to have lived to the age of 90! Most females live for about 50 years and males live for about 30 years.

How do orcas behave?

Behaviour can differ from one pod to another but certain activities are common among almost all orcas.

Pod structure

Unusually for mammals, many pods of orcas stay together for life. The pod is made up of close relatives and is usually led by the mother. Female orcas can have very long lives so sometimes four generations live together. In the Pacific Northwest, male and female resident orcas remain in the same pods they were born into but transient orcas do sometimes leave and can travel on their own.

Positions in a pod can be worked out by aggressive behaviour. Raking or tooth-scratching, when an orca runs its teeth over another orca's body, is common. Head-butting and tail-slapping can also be used.

Social clubs

Orcas form pods of 10 to 20 members but sometimes they join together to form superpods of up to 100 orcas. Researchers think that this is to make and maintain social relationships. The superpods are like social clubs where the orcas can meet other orcas and bond or find a mate. A lot of physical contact, rubbing of flippers, play, and swimming together takes place.

KILLERS OF HUMANS?

Orcas are also known as "killer whales". Up until the mid-1960s they were feared by humans and were often shot. However, there have been no records of a human being killed by an orca in the wild. In fact, orcas have helped humans who have been attacked by sharks. In captivity, there have been cases of orcas attacking their trainers. In 2010, a trainer was drowned when an orca pulled her under the water.

This orca pod is swimming in the Icy Strait in Alaska.

Communication

Researchers use underwater microphones to record the sounds made by resident orcas in the Pacific Northwest. By listening to the pulsed calls, they have discovered that different pods have different dialects. A dialect is a way of communicating that is carried out by a particular group in a particular area. Some orca pods use some of the same calls. These pods are known as clans. Orcas are one of very few mammals apart from humans that use dialects.

Orcas make different types of sounds for different reasons:

Type of call	Reason
Clicks	Used in echolocation to learn about surroundings and find prey.
Pulsed calls	Used to keep pods together and coordinate with other orcas.
Whistles	Used during social activities.

Orcas sometimes slap their tails on the ocean surface and this is known as fluke slapping or lob-tailing.

Common orca activities

Spyhopping, breaching, and fluke and pectoral slaps are all common orca behaviours. Spyhopping is when orcas raise their heads above water to see what's going on around them – particularly useful when hunting. Orcas breach by rising all the way out of the water, twisting around, and returning with a splash. Orcas slap their flukes or pectoral fins on the water to show aggression but sometimes also in play.

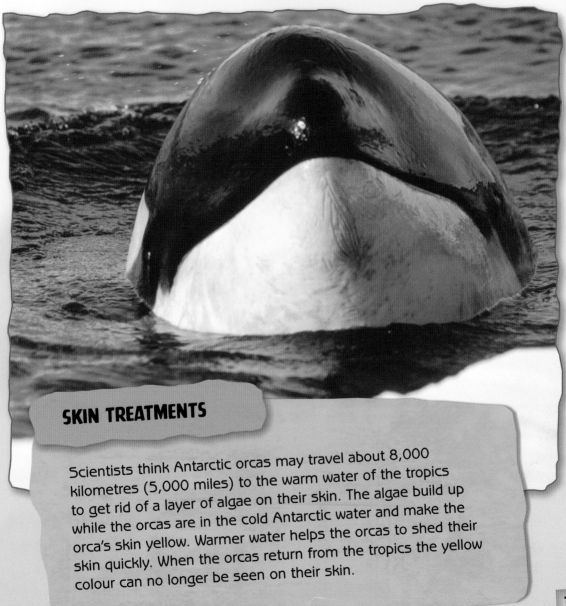

SKIN TREATMENTS

Scientists think Antarctic orcas may travel about 8,000 kilometres (5,000 miles) to the warm water of the tropics to get rid of a layer of algae on their skin. The algae build up while the orcas are in the cold Antarctic water and make the orca's skin yellow. Warmer water helps the orcas to shed their skin quickly. When the orcas return from the tropics the yellow colour can no longer be seen on their skin.

A DAY IN THE LIFE OF AN ORCA

An orca's day is made up of hunting, feeding, playing, and snoozing.

FEEDING TIME

Up to 60 per cent of a resident orca's day is spent looking for and eating food. Transient orcas can spend even longer hunting – up to 90 per cent of their day! The way orcas hunt for food depends on where they live. Working as a team, orcas can herd fish, catch seals and sea lions, or even attack large whales or sharks. Some orcas hunt on their own by sliding onto **ice floes** to eat penguins.

Young orcas spend time at a rubbing beach in Johnstone Strait, Canada.

FREE TIME

Many orcas play by tail or fin slapping or breaching, with younger orcas trying for the most adventurous spins and twists. Others have different ways to spend their time. Northern resident orcas visit rubbing beaches. They skim their bodies over pebbles at the bottom of the sea. They may do this to rub off old skin or maybe just for fun!

TIME FOR A SNOOZE

Humans do not have to think about breathing, but orcas have to choose to breathe because they would drown if they breathed under water. When it comes to sleeping, scientists think that an orca may rest one half of its brain at a time so that the other half can control its breathing. This usually happens for just a few minutes at a time but researchers have seen an orca sleep for eight hours before waking. Orcas can rest day or night and usually stay close to the surface while doing so.

When an orca comes up for air, its breath shows up as a fine mist.

How intelligent are orcas?

Intelligence is difficult to measure in animals. It usually refers to how animals hunt and maintain social relationships.

Hunting

Pods hunt through teamwork. Wave washing is one clever way of hunting prey. A pod of orcas dives under the ice. Then they use their tails to make a wave. This knocks a seal resting on ice into the water. Occasionally, the seal manages to escape but three times out of four, the orcas end up with a meal.

Orcas are sometimes called "wolves of the sea" because they hunt in packs like wolves hunt on land. The whale on the right is spyhopping (see page 31).

An orca can stun prey with its tail, which makes it easier to kill.

Orcas on the Peninsula Valdes in Argentina beach themselves to catch sea lions. They have worked out when Southern sea lions go there to have babies. Baby sea lions learning to swim are easier prey than adults!

Orcas sometimes hunt silently so the prey doesn't hear them coming. If they were to communicate as usual the prey would hear their clicks and calls. Instead it is thought that orcas practise their hunting routines before setting off for real. This means that each orca knows where the others will be.

Social skills

The fact that orcas are able to maintain peaceful family and social relationships also shows how intelligent they are. Play is a way for younger orcas to learn how to survive and for older animals it strengthens bonds.

Orcas in captivity have shown that they can learn to do many activities for the watching public. However, many people believe that orcas are too intelligent to be kept in captivity. They get bored and unhappy.

What threats do orcas face?

Pollution is a major problem for orcas because they are the top predators in the sea. Toxic chemicals from farms and industry are washed into the sea and get passed along the food chain. The largest amounts of chemicals end up in orca's blubber where they are difficult to break down. This can cause serious health problems. Orcas may not grow properly, be able to have healthy young, or be able to fight disease. Oil from oil spills can cause eye or skin irritation and is dangerous if swallowed.

Orcas can be damaged by whale-watching boats, so there are guidelines on how close boats should get to orcas.

Noise pollution

Orcas rely on their hearing more than any other sense. Noise pollution from boats, the marine industry, and the military is therefore a major problem. Loud noises can drown out the orcas' calls, making it hard for them to stay with their pod.

Stranding is when orcas are found on beaches. Researchers don't know for certain why this happens but it may be because an orca becomes ill or has an injury and can no longer keep up with the rest of the pod. However, stranding has also been caused by sonar used by the Navy. This disturbs the orcas' echolocation so they become confused and end up stranding themselves. Sonar can also make it difficult for orcas to find prey using echolocation.

IMPROVING AWARENESS

The Whale and Dolphin Conservation Society works hard to make industry and governments aware of the effects of noise pollution on orcas and other sea mammals. In 2012, it criticized a well-known research institute for carrying out underwater experiments with an airgun near Antarctica because of the harmful effect the high noise levels would have on whales and dolphins.

Fishing

Orcas are sometimes injured or killed after getting caught in fishing gear. Purse-seining is a type of fishing that uses a huge circular net to catch fish like mackerel. Many other types of fish – and orcas – can get caught in the net, too. Loss of prey because of overfishing by humans is another threat to orcas. Salmon and cod are common in orca diets as well as human ones. Fishermen themselves can also sometimes blame orcas for damage to expensive fishing gear and loss of their catch. There have been reports of orcas being shot as a result.

INGRID VISSER (BORN 1966)

Ingrid Visser is a marine biologist whose research helped the New Zealand government to reclassify the New Zealand orca to the level of "nationally critical", which means it is **endangered**. She has studied orcas since 1992 and has helped with research projects around the world. Visser teaches people about orcas by appearing in television programmes, giving talks, and writing about orcas.

Captivity and whaling

For many years, orcas were captured and taken to parks and dolphinariums to perform for the public. Fewer orcas are captured now, but sometimes rescued animals can be taken into captivity to provide another animal from which to **breed**. **Conservationists** try to prevent any more orcas being taken into captivity because captive orcas live less natural lives.

Orcas used to be hunted on a small scale for their meat and blubber but less so nowadays. A small number of orcas are still legally hunted for their meat by some Arctic tribes.

Captive orcas do not live as long as wild orcas. They only live into their 20s rather than 30s (males) or 50s (females).

How can people help orcas?

The more scientists learn about orcas, the more they will be able to protect these animals. Unfortunately, it is very difficult to study orcas because they live in oceans. Orcas can be tagged to learn more about where they go, but there is a danger that an orca may be injured when a dart gun is used to attach the transmitter. Also transmitters may not last very long. Orcas can be tracked by the calls they make, but researchers have to get close enough to use underwater microphones.

Learn all you can about orcas and the difficulties they face in the wild. Perhaps you could donate some pocket money or even sponsor an orca.

Conservation organizations

Conservation organizations not only research orcas but also try to make people more aware of the threats that sea mammals face in the wild. Simple things, such as not leaving litter at the beach, can help to protect orca habitats. Oil spills can cause problems for orcas and their habitats. There are ongoing efforts to speed up the clean and rescue times after a spill.

FREE MORGAN

In June 2010, a very ill orca was found off the coast of the Netherlands. Morgan (as she is now known) was supposed to be returned to the wild once she was well, but this has not happened. She has been sent to an amusement park in Spain to be used for captive breeding and performing for the public. Some conservation groups have campaigned to get Morgan released into the wild. Others have argued that past attempts to return orcas to the wild have failed and that Morgan will have a better life in captivity. What do you think?

Here, researchers in Antarctica watch an orca spyhopping.

What does the future hold for orcas?

Healthy adult orcas have no natural predators apart from humans. There are many conservation groups around the world already working to protect orcas and their habitats. Orcas are protected under UK and European Union law and under US law certain orca groups are also protected. However, more needs to be done. The level of pollution in our oceans must be reduced and people need to follow the rules on whale-watching activities. Learning more about orcas can help to focus conservation efforts.

Endangered mammals

It is difficult to know whether orcas are endangered because they are generally difficult to count. It is not even certain how many species there are. Certain populations of orcas can be considered endangered, however. The southern resident orcas that live in the Pacific Ocean around San Juan Islands and the Puget Sound were placed on the US endangered species list in 2005. There are thought to be under 100 orcas in this population. There is now a protected area for these orcas.

It is important that we don't allow orcas to die out. They deserve their place in the natural world. The more young people get involved in their protection, the better. Every little bit helps.

THE PACIFIC NORTHWEST

Orcas living in the Pacific Northwest are the most studied orcas anywhere. Researchers have been following orcas in the Pacific Ocean for over 30 years. They can recognize the orcas and have named them by giving them a letter and number, such as L12.

It is hoped that in the future there will be more protection for the amazing orca.

Species profile

Species: orca

Latin name: *Orcinus orca*

Length: 4.6 to 8 metres (15 to 26 feet) for females; 5 to 9 metres (16.4 to 29 ½ feet) for males

Weight: 3.8 to 8 tonnes for females; 5.6 to 9 tonnes for males

Habitat: all the world's oceans

Diet: fish, squid, penguins, other sea mammals such as seals, sea lions, or smaller whales

Number of young: Orcas usually give birth to one calf every three to five years. Pregnancy lasts 15 to 18 months.

Life expectancy in the wild (average): around 50 years for females; around 30 years for males

melon

blowhole

white patch behind eye

sharp teeth

strong jaw

dorsal fin

pectoral fin

saddle patch

light underside

flukes

Glossary

adaptation body part or behaviour of an organism that helps it survive in a particular habitat

blubber thick layer of fat on a sea mammal's body

breed mate and produce young

captive kept in parks or dolphinariums rather than being allowed to roam free

cetacean name for whales, dolphins, and porpoises

classification sorting of living things into groups

conservationist someone who helps to protect animals, plants, and habitats

echolocation ability to find objects or prey by bouncing sounds off them

endangered describes a species that is in danger of dying out

food chain sequence in which one creature eats another, which eats another, and so on

food web network of intertwined food chains

habitat natural environment of a living thing

horizontal being on the same flat level, like the horizon

ice floe flat area of floating ice

interdependence way in which all of the living things in a habitat and the habitat itself rely on each other for survival

mammal animal that has a backbone, has fur or hair, gives birth to live young, and feeds its young on milk from the mother

marine living in or of the sea

migrate move from one place to another, often at particular times of year

plankton small plants and animals that live in seawater

pod group of whales

pollution harmful waste that can end up in the sea

resident type of orca that spends most of their lives in the same pod in one area and eat mainly fish

resistance force that pushes back when something tries to move forward

social living in groups or communities, in which relationships are maintained

sonar pulses of sound that are used to find prey or learn about surroundings. Machines used by the navy and other organizations can also send out signals similar to those used by orcas.

species group of similar living things that can mate with each other

suckle take milk from a mother's body

transient type of orca that lives in the Pacific Northwest. They eat sea mammals and travel more than residents to find food.

vertical upright, or going straight up and down

wean encourage a pup to eat food other than its mother's milk

YOUR MINDFUL
Pregnancy

**meditations and practices for a stress-free,
happy, and healthy pregnancy**

Sarah Rudell Beach

CICO BOOKS
LONDON NEW YORK

To Abby and Liam,
I'm so lucky to be your mom

Published in 2021 by CICO Books
An imprint of Ryland Peters & Small Ltd

20–21 Jockey's Fields   341 E 116th St
London WC1R 4BW   New York, NY 10029

www.rylandpeters.com

10 9 8 7 6 5 4 3 2 1

ISBN: 978-1-78249-885-8

Printed in China

Commissioning editor: Kristine Pidkameny
Senior editor: Carmel Edmonds
Senior designer: Emily Breen
Art director: Sally Powell
Head of production: Patricia Harrington
Publishing manager: Penny Craig
Publisher: Cindy Richards

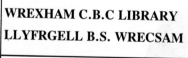

contents

introduction

Congratulations! Whether you've been hearing congratulations for months now, or if your pregnancy is still a closely guarded secret, I'm honored to offer my well wishes and blessings to you.

Pregnancy is a unique time in our life, one filled with a variety of emotions and a lot of changes in our bodies, our relationships, and even our sense of self. It's a time when our self-care, which is always important, takes on a special significance as we eat, sleep, and breathe for two. In the early stages of your pregnancy, your body reminds you of this need to slow down and nurture yourself through the hormone-induced fatigue that often has you falling asleep on the couch by 8pm!

I invite you to think of this book in your hands right now as another invitation to self-care. Becoming a mother, whether for the first or sixth time, is a significant change—one we need to face with lots of reserves of patience and empathy, and with a lot of skills in our wellness toolkit. Mindfulness can be a powerful ally for you in your motherhood journey.

My mindfulness and motherhood journey

To me, mindfulness and motherhood are deeply intertwined. While I had certainly heard of mindfulness prior to becoming a mother, I didn't begin to practice it until I was a mom. For me, becoming a mother was an amazing, powerful, and overwhelming experience. After years of feeling relatively in control of my schedule, my emotions, and my home (not to mention my sleep!), new motherhood presented an opportunity to be with uncertainty, unpredictability, and unexpected emotions. I discovered I needed a whole new set of skills to manage the changes in my life, as even the most beautiful and desired gifts (my dear daughter and, a few years later, my delightful son) often usher in a sense of feeling unsettled and unmoored.

I offer the words and practices in this book as a gift to you, a fellow mother embarking on an amazing, profound, and sometimes challenging journey. Discovering mindfulness when my children were infants, and deepening my practice into their toddlerhood, literally changed my life. I transformed how I interacted with my children (long story short: a lot more patience and a lot less frustration), how I navigated my own thoughts and emotions, and how I communicated with my partner as we sought to raise these beautiful humans as lovingly and intentionally as we could.

While I trust that the path I walked was the path I needed to be on, I often think about how my early years of motherhood may have been different had I known sooner the mindfulness practices that I will share with you in this book. I wonder how I may have approached my pregnancy differently, how I may have labored differently, and certainly how I may have adjusted to those first few weeks and months of motherhood differently. I hope that this book empowers you to cultivate a mindfulness practice for yourself as a resource now, something that you can call upon when you need it throughout your pregnancy and in readiness for your life as a mother.

Pregnancy, while it may feel like it lasts forever, is a brief portion of your motherhood journey, but, if you'll excuse the pun, it's a fertile time for you to learn new practices and perspectives as you transition to a new life stage. It's a time to bond with your baby, to connect more deeply to yourself, and to cultivate the skills and practices that support greater calm, joy, and ease. Beginning, or deepening, your mindfulness practice at this time of your life will serve you, and your children, for many years to come.

I wish you lots of love on the journey!

How to use this book

In the chapters that follow, I will introduce you to simple mindfulness practices that you can incorporate into your day. In Chapter 1, you'll learn how to make mindfulness a habit during your pregnancy, one that you can sustain throughout your motherhood journey. In Chapter 2, you'll discover specific practices that can help you navigate the stresses of pregnancy and support your physical and emotional health. In Chapter 3, I'll offer a variety of exercises that will promote bonding between you and your baby, well before she enters the world. In Chapter 4, we'll explore the ways that you can mindfully prepare for labor, and you'll learn mindfulness techniques that can support you as you give birth. Finally, in Chapter 5, you'll discover mindfulness practices that will help you bond with your baby and adjust to new motherhood.

The book, therefore, follows the timeline of your pregnancy journey, but feel free to "skip around" as you explore the practices that will be most helpful to you. If you're new to mindfulness, I recommend you begin with Chapter 1, as it contains many introductory practices and meditations to get you started on the basics.

This book is intended to provide both guidance and inspiration for your mindfulness practice. You'll discover lots of different ways to bring mindfulness into your day. Think of this book as a menu, not an all-you-can-eat buffet. Sample the exercises that appeal to you, experiment with them in the laboratory of your own life, and see what works for you. If a particular practice brings you some ease and comfort, you can come back for seconds.

Honor your own feelings and intuition—if a particular practice doesn't feel right to you, feel free to modify it or not do it at all. You can't do all of the exercises every day, nor should you even try! See if you can approach mindfulness with an attitude of playfulness—play with these practices, see what resonates with you, and consider how you can integrate mindfulness into your life as an important component of your self-care.

chapter 1

BECOMING MORE
Mindful

BASIC PRACTICES AND TECHNIQUES TO PROMOTE SELF-CARE

Paying attention is a skill, one that we cultivate through deliberate practice. If we want to be more present, and to be able to move through our lives with greater calm and ease, we need to practice. Just as we don't become better cooks by simply reading recipes, we cannot become more mindful just by reading about mindfulness.

We need to practice.

what is mindfulness?

You probably hear about mindfulness a lot these days; it's gotten quite a bit of attention lately for its ability to help us manage our stress. And while mindfulness is a powerful tool for meeting stress, it is, fundamentally, a way of paying attention.

Paying careful attention to the present moment

As a human being with a human brain, you've probably already experienced how difficult it can be to pay attention! In fact, researchers say that many of us today live in a state they call "continuous partial attention": instead of focusing on one thing at a time, we try to place our attention on many things all at once (such as washing the dishes while planning tomorrow's meeting in your head and also wondering if you need to pick up milk at the store and *also* trying to respond to the question your husband just asked you). It's exhausting!

With mindfulness, we train ourselves to **pay careful attention to the present moment**. We bring our attention to what we are doing, thinking, saying, or feeling as we do, think, say, or feel it. We focus on being *here*, in this body, in this moment.

Curiosity

We also pay attention in a special way: **with curiosity**. As adults, we sometimes look at the world without really seeing it. We've probably walked the same route from the front door to the car hundreds of times, literally on autopilot. We probably don't notice the small details like the exact patterns of leaves on the grass, or the squirrel running up the tree. With mindfulness, we bring curiosity to our experience: what does the outside world look like today? Or, upon waking in the morning, we may think we know exactly how our day is going to go, and we may even feel a sense of dread or irritation as we think about heading into work. But with a little curiosity, we can be more open to our experience. We can acknowledge that we actually don't know how the day is going to turn out. We can allow things to unfold as they are, rather than being stuck in the stories in our head.

Non-judgment

This means that when we pay attention mindfully, we also pay attention **non-judgmentally**. Once you start paying attention to your thoughts, you'll likely notice that you spend a lot of time judging. There's no reason to be upset with yourself for thinking this way; it's what your brain was designed to do, after all. It's your brain's job to judge things ("Is this safe?", "Am I okay?", "Should I approach or avoid?"). But sometimes all that judging actually makes you feel pretty miserable, especially when you're turning your judgment on yourself.

With mindfulness, you begin to notice the judging commentary in your mind, and you learn practices for interrupting those judgments and for seeing things more clearly. In fact, you may have noticed yourself already engaging in a lot of self-judgment in your pregnancy, telling yourself you're not eating healthily enough or exercising enough or something else. These thoughts are quite normal, but also not very helpful! As you move through the exercises in this book, you'll learn techniques for working with your worries and not being so self-critical.

Positivity

In addition to paying attention to the present moment, with curiosity and awareness of our judgments, mindfulness also includes the **cultivation of positive mind-states**, including joy, gratitude, and empathy. These positive traits improve both our mental and physical well-being, and, as you can imagine, are quite important for us as we navigate our journey through pregnancy and motherhood.

A mindful moment

While all the explanations on the previous pages are multi-faceted and perhaps seem complex, mindfulness is fundamentally simple—it is about **being present**, in this moment. When we are present, our capacity to pay attention, to notice judgments, to be open and curious, and to incline the mind to positive states is naturally cultivated. And the best way to do that is to practice—in this moment. Try the exercise below.

As you are reading these words right now, check in with your present-moment experience. Notice where you are sitting. Can you feel the places where your body is making contact with the surface that's supporting you?

Look up from this page and take in your surroundings. Take a moment to fully see the space you occupy right now—what colors or familiar objects do you see?

Pause for a moment to listen. What sounds can you hear?

Finally, take two slow breaths with full awareness. What does it feel like in your body, right now, as you breathe?

If you've never practiced mindfulness before, congratulations! You just spent a moment in mindful awareness.

In truth, you've had LOTS of moments of mindfulness already in your life. You've had experiences where you were fully present and took in what was happening with open curiosity (think of moments like your first kiss, or a time when you were deeply engaged in a creative project, or the day you first learned you were pregnant). While these moments may differ in their emotional charge, they shared the quality of **mindful attention**; in fact, you can probably close your eyes right now and remember the way your body felt in that moment, and you may even remember the sounds and smells of the experience, too.

When we deliberately cultivate a mindfulness practice, we can have more of these moments of presence and attention. And the research tells us that there are lots of benefits of being more mindful, such as reducing our stress and feeling happier.

we focus on being
here, in this body,
in this moment

Mindfulness and meditation: what's the difference?

Mindfulness teachers might define these terms slightly differently, but it's helpful for us to orient ourselves to how I will be using them in this book. Mindfulness is, as defined earlier, a way of paying attention. It is a much broader concept than meditation; mindfulness is a way we can approach the totality of our experience.

We can walk mindfully,
speak mindfully,
eat mindfully,
drive mindfully,
and play mindfully.

By meditation, I mean the formal practice of setting aside some time in our day to eliminate other distractions and focus our attention inward—on the breath, the body, and the mind. It's during this concentrated practice that we cultivate our ability to be more present throughout our day, i.e. to be mindful.

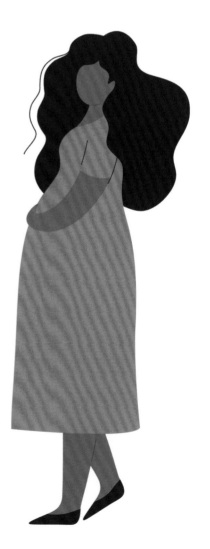

What mindfulness is not

Before we turn to more specific practices to help you have a mindful and joyful pregnancy, let me offer a few things that mindfulness is *not*, as I think it helps to clarify more what it actually *is*.

Mindfulness is not *not* thinking

One of the biggest misconceptions about mindfulness is that it means we must "clear our minds" and stop our thoughts. But you can no more stop thinking than you can stop breathing. Thinking is just what your mind does. With mindfulness, the goal is to bring greater awareness to your thoughts, instead of being completely wrapped up in them. Once you can start to recognize the habitual patterns in your thinking, you can approach your everyday life with greater insight and clarity.

Mindfulness is not being calm or relaxed all the time

Another misconception about mindfulness is that it will make you calm and relaxed each and every time you do it. Often, mindfulness *is* relaxing; it's a nice side-effect of the practice. But really, the purpose of mindfulness isn't to relax; it is to pay attention to your present-moment experience. And sometimes, that experience is unpleasant. Sometimes you're just not relaxed. That's okay. Notice what it feels like to not be relaxed. Eventually, you'll start to have a better sense of the practices that help you feel grounded and calm and stable, and you can call upon those when they're needed. But you'll still have very human moments of losing your cool or letting your thoughts and emotions overwhelm you, because you'll still be very human. And the gift of mindfulness is that it provides us with powerful tools for navigating the human condition.

Mindfulness is not religious

Mindfulness does have its origins in religious traditions, primarily the teachings of the Buddha. But it is completely possible to practice mindfulness in a way that is secular, and doesn't conflict with your religious views (if you have them). While Buddhism and Hinduism say a great deal about mindfulness, so did Christian mystics and Roman stoics and a lot of nonreligious philosophers. The mindfulness taught and practiced in the West today is based on scientific research that indicates that these attention practices can actually alter the structure of the brain in ways that promote greater focus and concentration and improved emotional regulation.

Mindfulness is not never planning for the future

Focusing on the present moment doesn't mean you can't ever envision or think about future moments; life would be pretty difficult if that were the case! The problem, however, is that on a busy day, we're often thinking about the past, the present, and the future all at once, as we rush into our morning meeting still worried about the tasks we didn't finish yesterday and mentally ticking off all the things we need to do today. Mindfulness is really about single-tasking as opposed to multi-tasking (see page 48); you can write your to-do list, and just write your to-do list. You can be fully present with the act of planning your day. And then you can be fully present as you begin to put that plan into action.

Mindfulness is not being okay with everything

Mindfulness also doesn't mean you have to be okay with everything because "that's just how it is." Mindfulness is not passivity; in fact, our mindful awareness can compel us to take action to alleviate suffering when we are unencumbered enough to see it. I prefer to think of mindfulness as something that helps me determine, with awareness and clarity, the things over which I have control, and those I don't.
As the 8th-century monk Shantideva supposedly said,

> *"If you can solve your problem, why are you worrying?*
> *If you cannot solve it, why are you worrying?"*

Mindfulness helps us see our problems clearly and gives us the ability to take wise action when needed, and allows us to soften into the things we cannot change.

beginning your mindfulness practice

One of the most important things about mindfulness is that it is a *practice*. It's something we must cultivate—we can't just read a book, decide to appreciate mindfulness and peacefulness and attentiveness from now on, and expect things to change, any more than we can read a book about exercise, decide to *appreciate* sweat and movement, and expect to be fitter. We have to practice. Mindfulness is like a muscle, something that will grow stronger the more we use it. The more we practice pausing, the better we will get at it. The more aware we become of our thought patterns, the less we'll be driven by them, and we'll be able to change some of our reactive habits that aren't serving us very well. And, according to the research, we'll experience less stress and greater joy. All of these things can help you find greater enjoyment in your pregnancy and motherhood, and help you be the mother you want to be.

When to practice

If you are new to mindfulness practice, I recommend starting with just a few minutes of formal practice each day (3–5 minutes, maximum). Choose a time of day that will work best for you, when you know you won't be interrupted, and when you will be alert. For many of us, this is first thing in the morning, but it could also be during your lunch break at work, or in your car before driving home, or right before you go to bed.

As best you can, try to practice at the same time each day, as this will make it easier to establish mindfulness as a daily habit. Consistency of practice is far more important than the duration of your practice. Just five minutes a day of breathing in attentive silence will help you cultivate greater calm, focus, and patience, *and you always have five minutes.*

mindfulness is like a muscle that grows stronger the more we use it

Finding the time

When you're really busy, you might think taking five minutes to meditate just isn't worth it, because then you'll be even more behind schedule. But we often "earn back" the time we spend in mindfulness practice. Spending a few minutes in quiet stillness creates a calm and focus that will help you be more productive and efficient throughout your day.

And although it's important to create time for your mindfulness practice in your day, it's also important to not make mindfulness just another item on your to-do list, a chore that must be completed. Mindfulness should be a "get to," not a "have to." Think of ways that you can ritualize your practice—maybe lighting a candle or listening to soothing music—so that your time feels special and set apart from the rest of your day. Allow your time for mindfulness to be a gift you give yourself. You are on for most of your day—taking in information, responding to the world, moving through space, navigating your surroundings—and all that time on takes its toll on your energy, clarity, and presence. Think of meditation as your time to *not* be on—to not have to respond, engage, or move. To just be.

allow your time for mindfulness to be a gift you give yourself

meditation postures
in pregnancy

The typical image most people have of meditation is someone seated
in a cross-legged lotus pose, with a straight spine—and often an oddly
beatific smile on their face. My approach to mindfulness and meditation
postures is, literally, a relaxed one. If the lotus position works for you,
great! But as your body continues to change during pregnancy, you may
find you need to experiment with various positions and postures for
your formal practice.

The most important thing to consider in your meditation posture is your **comfort**.
Sitting in meditation is not about enduring pain! The goal is to find a position that
promotes both relaxation *and* alertness—two states we don't often associate with
each other. You want your muscles and body to be able to release tension, but you
don't want to be so relaxed that you end up falling
asleep! (Though if you do fall asleep, that's okay! See
page 59.) Know that it is always okay to shift your
posture in formal meditation if you need to
relieve discomfort or feel more awake. Just
make that movement in full awareness,
noticing what it feels like after you make
the adjustment.

Sitting

For seated meditation, you can either use a chair or sit on the floor on a cushion cross-legged or with legs outstretched. If you use a chair, sit with both feet touching the floor; depending on the style of the chair, you can rest your back on the backrest, or you can sit upright. Your seat should be no lower than your knees—this way, your seat and your knees form a tripod to keep you balanced. If you sit on a cushion, try to position it so that your tailbone and sit-bones—the rounded bones at the bottom of your pelvis— are elevated (and, if you're sitting cross-legged, so that your knees touch the floor).

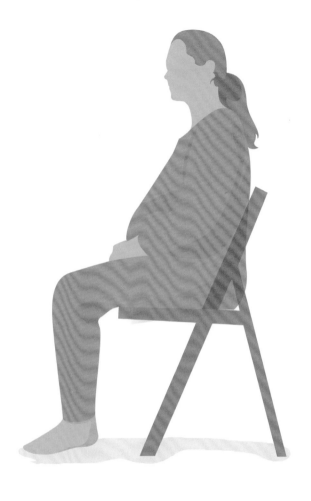

Lying down

You may find it more comfortable to lie down when you practice, especially
if you're experiencing back or tailbone pain during your pregnancy. In the first
trimester, lying on your back may work well, either with your legs fully extended,
or with your knees bent and your feet closer to your buttocks (this latter pose is
helpful if you experience back pain). As your pregnancy progresses, it will probably
feel more comfortable to lie on your side and you may find it supportive to place
a pillow between your legs. Please always prioritize your comfort in whatever
posture you choose, and be sure to follow the advice of your healthcare provider
about safe positions for sleeping and lying down.

Standing or walking

Mindfulness meditation does not need to be a completely still activity. You could try standing —keeping your eyes open to help you balance, as your center of gravity changes in pregnancy. You could also practice walking meditation—see page 37.

What to do with your hands

Again, the guidance here is comfort. In a seated posture, you could place your hands in your lap or on your thighs. In a lying down position, you can place your hands on your stomach, or you could have them at your side. I'd like to offer that during pregnancy, placing your hands on your heart or your belly is an especially lovely way to connect to your baby in these moments of presence and awareness.

simple meditation practices

The following techniques can form the basis of your mindfulness practices. I invite you to try them all and see which ones seem most suited to you.

Mindfulness of the breath

Mindfulness almost always begins with the breath, as it is always available to us; we're always breathing! Try the practice opposite. You may choose to record it so that you can listen with your eyes closed.

tip

BREATHING TECHNIQUE

You may find it supportive to breathe in through your nose and out through your mouth, as this can also be a helpful breathing practice during labor. In general, however, the best recommendation is to simply let your breath be natural: notice breathing happening, instead of "trying" to breathe.

Shortness of breath

As your pregnancy progresses, you might find deep breathing to be a bit more difficult, as your growing baby pushes up against your lungs. Please know that you do not need to force deep breathing—your body breathes for you all day just fine without you trying to control it! If your breath feels shallow, then simply notice that, without assuming that you are "doing it wrong." You may notice that the breath becomes deeper the longer you practice, or begins to slow on its own. If that happens, just observe it and notice how it feels.

For this practice, just for right now, notice your breathing. You don't need to control your breath or breathe in any particular way. Just bring your attention to your breath.

See what you notice about your breath: is it fast or slow? Does it feel warm or cool? Can you notice the sensations of your breath in your nose? In your chest? In your belly?

Do you notice if you're trying to control your breath? If so, see if you can just let breathing happen on its own, perhaps paying special attention to the pause at the end of each in-breath and at the end of each out-breath.

See if you can breathe like this, with full awareness, for about a minute. You could try simply saying to yourself "breathing in" each time you breathe in, and "breathing out" each time you breathe out. You could also count each breath, or perhaps it helps to place a hand on your chest or your belly and notice the gentle movement of your body as you breathe.

When your mind wanders away to something else (which it will), just bring your attention back to your breath.

If you'd like, you can close your eyes as you continue to focus on the physical sensations of breathing.

When you're ready, allow your eyes to gently open, and take a moment to notice how you feel.

Mindfulness of your changing body

Another supportive, and often relaxing, mindfulness practice is the body scan, in which you anchor your attention on the physical sensations in the body. For this practice, you can read the description below, and then lie down (either on your back or your side) to do the body scan. You may also choose to record the practice so that you can listen to it as you do the scan.

As you settle into a lying down position, take a moment to check in with your body. What sensations do you notice right away? Your attention might be immediately drawn to areas of discomfort or tension, and if that is the case, is it possible to relax your muscles or shift your position slightly to make yourself more comfortable?

Beginning with your feet, gently sweep your attention over your body, noticing things like warmth or coolness, tingling or buzzing, movement or stillness. As you focus on your legs and lower body, pay special attention to your ankles… knees… thighs… all the muscles of your legs. Take a moment to be grateful for your legs supporting you and helping you move through the world each day, and enjoy this moment of offering your lower body a rest.

*Continue to bring your attention to your hips and your belly. What do
you notice? While your pregnancy impacts all of your body, you probably
especially feel it here. What new sensations or movements do you notice?
If you are far enough along in your pregnancy, place a hand on your belly
and see if you can feel your baby. Take a moment to be grateful for your
hips and belly and all the amazing transformations occurring in your body.*

*Allow your attention to move up to your chest and your arms. Can you
notice your breath? Can you let your arms fully relax? Spend a moment
in gratitude for all the work your heart and lungs and arms do for you
all day.*

*As you bring your attention to your neck and your face, see where you can
soften and relax. Can you release all the tension in your face—around
your eyes, in your jaw, from your forehead? Thank your facial muscles for
all the talking and expressing they have done for you today, and now let
them rest.*

*Right now, your body is a place of amazing transformation, with your baby
growing in your belly, and all the systems of your body working to support
your baby (and you). Take a few breaths to appreciate the wonder of your
body and how, already, it is helping you nurture your precious child.*

Mindful listening

In mindfulness practice, we often speak of having an anchor—something to hold your attention in place amid a lot of distractions. In the exercise on pages 28–29, your breath was your anchor, bringing you back to the present moment. In this practice, you'll focus on sound as an anchor.

Sitting here, in this moment, what can you hear?

Can you notice sounds in the room, perhaps a ticking clock or the whirring of a fan? Can you notice sounds from outside the room or even outdoors, perhaps distant traffic or the chirping of birds? Can you hear your breath?

If you find a particular sound that feels soothing or relaxing to attend to, let your attention rest there, and when your mind wanders, gently invite it back to noticing the sound.

You could also experiment with allowing your attention to take in the entire soundscape around you, not necessarily focusing on any sound in particular. You can just let the sounds come to you, noticing how they come and go of their own accord.

After a few moments of mindful listening, pause and notice how you feel.

mindfulness of thoughts

Mindfulness doesn't mean not thinking. Once you practice for even a few minutes, you will realize just how much thinking your busy mind does! Many people beginning a mindfulness practice think that *thinking* means they are doing it wrong. But here's the secret: noticing that you are thinking IS the practice.

Consider how much of your day you are thinking without even realizing it! Researchers estimate we have somewhere between 50,000 and 70,000 thoughts in a day. Most of those are automatic, habitual thoughts or mind-wandering—I'm sure you can think of a time when you have pulled yourself back from being "lost in thought" and were startled by how random or nonsequential your thoughts were.

Label your thoughts

When you notice thinking during your mindfulness practice (or at any time during the day, really), you can simply note "thinking." You could even give a more specific label to your mental activity: "planning," "remembering," "worrying," "justifying," "blaming," etc. You don't need to actually engage the thought. Just observe it, the same way you might observe a sound you hear or a sensation in your body. See what happens to the thought—does it go away, or does it stick around? Either is fine; you're just noticing it, without having to get entangled in it.

What you may come to realize is just how persuasive and intense thoughts can be in the moment, but after just a few seconds of seeing them clearly, they lose a bit of their hold on you. You don't need to act on them right away.

The more you practice mindfulness, you might start to recognize specific thought patterns, some of which may be helpful, others not so much. You can start to interrupt the negative thoughts before they get out of hand.

Mindfully working with thoughts

Some helpful ways of working with thoughts in mindfulness practice are imagining the thoughts as:

- Clouds passing through the sky
- Balloons drifting up into the air
- Boats floating down a river
- The cars of a train passing by
- Bubbles breaking to the surface of the water

In all these cases, your job is simply to observe the movement. You start to realize that thoughts, sensations, and emotions all eventually pass on their own, and you can choose how to observe and relate to them. You can also use the technique of returning to the breath.

notice the breath

back to the breath

mind wanders

realize mind has wandered

All the judging

As you notice your thoughts more, you may notice a lot of judgments about other people—and yourself. You may start to notice just how much of your time is spent wishing things were somehow *different* than they are in the moment.

It's okay when you notice this. In a way, this is what your mind was designed to do—to judge situations and determine if they are safe or if you should avoid them. But all this judging tends to get in the way of us truly experiencing a moment or enjoying it, and it often leads to a lot of self-criticism. When you notice a judgment, such as "I can't believe I took such a long nap today and I didn't get anything done" or "I can't believe I didn't let myself nap today and worked so much my body aches," take a moment to notice the judgment. Is it true? Is it actually true? Can you offer yourself a bit of kindness in this moment instead?

Instead of judging the present moment, can you find a way to be with it? Even if it's not what you chose, or how you wanted things to unfold, it's what is here right now. You can choose how to be with it.

mindfulness throughout your day

In addition to formal mindfulness practices like paying attention to your breath, your body, or sound, you can bring mindfulness to the things you do throughout your day. You might be amazed at the small things you can notice when you start to pay more careful attention to even the most mundane tasks.

Over the next few days, see what it's like to bring your full attention to the following activities:

- Brushing your teeth
- Washing dishes
- Making your bed
- Folding laundry
- Making dinner
- Washing your hands

Notice what it's like to bring your open, curious, nonjudgmental attention to these daily actions. Do you tend to rush through these tasks? Does your mind wander as you do them? Just as in the other exercises, when your mind wanders, see if you can gently bring your attention back to the task in front of you. See what it's like to have your attention fully focused on one task.

Mindful walking

Walking is a great form of exercise while you are pregnant, and you can make walking part of your mindfulness practice. See what it's like to leave your headphones at home and simply go for a walk in your neighborhood with an intention to truly pay attention. What does it feel like to move your body? Can you be mindful of each step, noticing how you place your front foot on the ground as your back foot prepares to step forward? What sounds can you hear? What colors and sights can you see? What do you smell? Can you feel the outside air on your skin?

A fun way to walk mindfully during your pregnancy is to imagine seeing your neighborhood as your baby might. What new things can you notice? What sights will you point out to your baby when he's able to join you (on the outside) for a walk?

Being curious

A core quality we seek to cultivate in mindfulness practice is curiosity. We so often approach the world with a "been there, done that" attitude; our days can feel so routine and familiar that we don't even consider the possibility that things might be slightly different from day to day. This often shows up in our interactions with others ("I know exactly what she's going to say!"), our work ("This meeting will be just like the one last week…"), and the ways in which we go about our day on autopilot. Have you ever driven somewhere, only to realize that you hadn't actually been paying attention to driving? What does it mean for us when we go through the rest of the day this way, too?

See if you can bring curiosity to your day today. Turn off the radio as you drive to work and notice the sights around you. Really see the rooms in your home as you walk through them. Fully listen to your partner at dinner. Consider how powerful this curious attention will be when you begin to share your days with your baby.

Expectations while you're expecting

As you practice bringing curiosity to your moment-to-moment experience, see if you can pay special attention to your expectations. In truth, our days are *full* of expectation—of what will happen next and how our day will unfold. It would be quite hard, in fact, to navigate through our day *without* expectation.

And there's probably a reason we refer to pregnancy as "expecting," because this is a time when your expectations are likely quite high—for yourself, your baby, your future. Again, this is completely normal… and something to notice. Expectations can be helpful guideposts as we move into the future if we are able to hold those expectations lightly. If we start to cling too tightly to a specific vision of how things are to unfold—our day, our labor, our baby's life, our life!—we can become easily frustrated by unmet expectations. Mindfulness is about finding a careful balance between our intentions for how we want to show up in the world, and how our life actually plays out.

When you notice expectation, which may come in the form of a daydream of what life at home with your baby will look like, a carefully detailed birth plan, or a vision of who your baby will be, simply pause and notice, "This is expectation." It's not bad or wrong that you have an expectation. In fact, take a moment to savor the love and positive intentions that are behind these expectations—your desire to provide your baby with a loving home, a safe birth, and a full life.

And then take a moment to remind yourself that those intentions can be realized in many ways. See if you can orient to the intention *behind* the expectation, rather than a specific version of how things need to, or should, unfold.

chapter 2

A MINDFUL
Pregnancy

MANAGING THE UPS AND DOWNS OF PREGNANCY

One of the most common pieces of advice given to pregnant women is to "avoid stress"—an admonition that often causes more stress! Research indicates that reducing stress levels is supportive for you and your baby, but please keep in mind that there are many other contributors to a healthy pregnancy. It's also helpful to remember that it's hard to "avoid stress," because it is often caused by things that are outside of your control. What you can work on minimizing is your response to stressful events and that is where your mindfulness practice is deeply supportive.

your mental well-being

We already know that our minds are constantly full of thoughts (see page 33). In and of themselves, thoughts are not a problem, but when they become worries they can create a lot of unnecessary stress. The practices on the following pages can support you during moments of tension and worry.

Mindfulness of worries

Pregnancy brings a lot of joy, and it can also bring a lot of worries. You may worry about your health, or your baby's health, or your finances… (I won't worry you by adding to the list!) Mindfulness can't eliminate worries, but it can provide you with helpful strategies for making the worries, well, less worrisome.

When you notice worried thoughts, try one or more of the following strategies:

- **Remind yourself that worries are normal.** It's your brain's job to keep you safe and alive, and one way it does that is by making sure you consider things like consequences and dangers. A healthy amount of concern over your health or about your baby is, in fact, an ancient evolutionary strategy designed to keep you well.

- **Thank your worries.** Given the above, you could try meeting your worries with gratitude. Sometimes I'll say to my worries (in my head): "Thank you for doing your best to keep me safe. But I've got this."

- **Write down your worries.** Worries can seem so much bigger when they're occupying so much space in your head. Spend a few moments journaling about the things that are worrying you. The act of putting them down on paper can help you unburden your mind.

- **Ask yourself, "How likely is this to happen?"** It seems there are so many dangers you are warned about in pregnancy, but many of them are statistically unlikely. While it's important to be informed, it's also important to keep a sense of perspective.

- **Ask yourself, "If this were to happen, how would I handle it?"** Happiness researchers have found that we often overestimate how devastating a negative life event would be, and we generally underestimate our ability to cope with that event. If it feels okay, take a moment to imagine the thing you're worried about actually happening, and consider the resources and strength that you have to meet it. This can help you "close the loop" on your worry and set it aside.

- **Acknowledge the worry.** When you notice a worry, say to yourself, "This is a worry," or even just, "Worrying, worrying." You don't need to engage the content of the worry; simply acknowledge that this is a moment of worry, and then place your hand on your heart and take a few deep breaths.

writing down worries can help you unburden your mind

- **Be kind to yourself.** After recognizing a moment of worry, check in with what you need. Would it help to take a few mindful breaths? Do you need a cup of tea? A nap? Offer yourself the kindness of tending to your needs.

- **Seek help if you need it.** If you are especially concerned about an aspect of your health or your baby's development, please do check in with your healthcare provider. If you feel some discomfort about reaching out (perhaps a sense of not wanting to bother them, or fearing you'll be seen as overly worried), I invite you to see this as a practice in advocating for yourself and for your baby. Your practitioner is there to support you, and can offer a wealth of information. Utilize the resources that are open to you.

Birth story blues

Once people find out that you are pregnant, they will probably tell you a birth story… and it is unlikely to be a pleasant and simple one. You may feel overwhelmed at times by all the unsolicited birth-storytelling from friends, relatives, and even complete strangers. If you find yourself on the receiving end of yet another horrific birth story, call upon your mindfulness practice. Take a deep breath and remind yourself that *it's not **your** story*. Can you assume that the person sharing this with you is motivated by a desire to support you, and not scare you? If the information starts to feel too overwhelming or upsetting, be honest about how you are feeling. You could say, "I'm glad that you trust me enough to share this story, but I notice that hearing it is making me feel a bit tense and nervous. Could we take a break from talking about this?" With this gentle reminder, most mothers will remember the times they were in your position and will hopefully take the hint.

If you happen to find yourself on the receiving end of a positive birth story, take a moment to savor it. Express your gratitude to the person for sharing their positive energy and intentions with you. How does it feel to hear a beautiful story about birth?

Story time

Humans are story-telling creatures, not just around campfires but all day long. It's like we're starring in the documentary of our own life, and we are providing constant narration. The problem with this continual story-telling is that it is often inaccurate. Instead of just capturing the raw footage of our day the way a camera would, our stories are full of assumptions, judgments, half-truths, and outright fabrications. And sometimes these inaccurate stories can lead to a lot of suffering.

See if, throughout your day, you can pause and notice when you are telling yourself a story. Researcher and author Brené Brown suggests the prompt,

"The story I'm telling myself right now is…"

For example, you might say, "The story I'm telling myself right now is that I will never be a good enough mother," or "The story I'm telling myself right now is that I will have failed at labor if I have a C-section." Just naming the story can disarm it a bit, in much the same way labeling our emotions takes away a bit of their charge. Once you've identified the story, you can find the plot holes. You can change the story to offer yourself a bit more grace and kindness. You can remind yourself that what ultimately matters is bringing your baby into the world, not necessarily the exact process by which it happens. You can remind yourself that you are reading this very book, cultivating practices that will support you in being the mother you wish to be.

Notice when you are telling yourself stories, and see if you can let your narrative support you, instead of hurt you.

You're already a good mother

A common worry during pregnancy (and throughout motherhood, if we're honest!) is whether we will be good mothers. Author Jodi Picoult has quipped that the fact that we worry about this in the first place is proof that we already *are* good mothers, and I remind myself of this frequently.

If this is your second or a subsequent pregnancy, you may be noticing this worry even more, as you navigate your fatigue, your healthcare appointments, and your preparations for a new baby amid caring for your child's needs. You may worry about being enough, or being able to attend to so many competing demands for your energy, attention, and love.

When you notice this worry about being a good mother arise, you can use the strategies on pages 43–44. But this worry in particular strikes at the heart of our vulnerabilities and doubts, and may need some special care. You can remind yourself that this worry itself is evidence of your dedication to your children and their well-being. (You may even find comfort, as I do, in the psychological research that tells us that what children need is a "good enough" mother, not a perfect one.)

You may also find the mantras or phrases below supportive. If one of them particularly resonates with you, say it silently to yourself, and then close your eyes, letting the words really sink in. Allow the phrase to not be just words. Allow them to be felt in your body, and notice what it feels like to offer yourself this kind reassurance.

"I am a good mother."

"I am doing the best I can, for myself and for my child(ren)."

"I am enough."

"This moment is hard, and that is okay."

"In this moment, my loving presence is enough."

"If it's hard for me, it's hard for other mothers, too."

Tension tamer

This is a fun exercise I often do with kids, but I find it's a helpful way for adults to relieve some stress, too!

In either a standing or seated position (see pages 25 and 27), take a deep breath in, and then tighten all the muscles of your face. Then make your hands into fists… and then release the muscles of your face and hands as you breathe out. Do this process again, noticing what it feels like when you are tense (maybe you already were!), and then noticing what it feels like to release tension.

Sometimes, we best understand relaxation in contrast to tension, and this can be a simple way to invite relaxation into the body.

Single-tasking

We seem to be obsessed with multi-tasking these days. We're expected to respond to emails while getting our work done or to make dinner while helping our kids with their homework. The problem is, multi-tasking is a computer word. Computers can perform multiple complicated tasks at one time; human brains cannot. We function best when we can focus on one thing at a time.

See if, just for today, you can experiment with single-tasking. When you make a meal, just make the meal, without also trying to plan tomorrow's meeting and making a phone call to schedule a playdate. When you drive, just drive. When you write an email, just write an email. See what you notice about your attention, your body, and your productivity when you single-task.

when you cook,
just cook

Mindful at work

We can bring mindfulness to all the moments of our day, our workday included!
If you are working during your pregnancy, you may be finding it hard to focus due
to fatigue or distraction about preparing for an upcoming maternity leave.

The following practices can help you to be more mindful at work:

- Set a timer on your phone to go off once an hour (or even every 30 minutes) as a reminder to stand up (if you spend much of your day seated), stretch, and breathe.

- Practice single-tasking at work; set a time for when you will answer emails, and then turn off your email notifications when you turn to a project that needs your full attention.

- Try to get outside at least once during the day to walk mindfully, perhaps at lunchtime

- Discuss your maternity leave plan with your supervisor and colleagues, so that you can ensure you are able to focus on your maternity leave without distractions from work.

You may notice a variety of emotions about your work during your pregnancy—worries about missing out on important projects, sadness or guilt about having to eventually return, joy about eventually returning, or worries about being at home without your work as a steady part of your day. All of these thoughts and emotions are completely normal. See if you can notice and label the thoughts without judgment (see page 35), or try the exercises for working with worries and emotions on pages 43–44 and 52–54.

your emotional well-being

You may notice that your emotions feel all over the place during pregnancy, due to the powerful combination of hormonal, physical, and lifestyle changes that are taking place for you right now. You may experience mood swings or heightened stress, and all of this is entirely normal (although it's important to speak to your healthcare provider if it becomes too overwhelming or begins to interfere with your everyday life).

Difficult emotions

Mindfulness offers us powerful strategies for working with strong and difficult emotions. It can't prevent those emotions from arising, but we wouldn't want it to, as our emotions are important sources of information about our present-moment experiences.

Come back to your body

When you notice yourself feeling overwhelmed by emotion, take a moment to pause and **notice your breath**. This is where the kind curiosity that we cultivate in our mindfulness practice can be especially supportive. Where in your **body** is this emotion? What does it **feel like**?

While emotions can be intense, they are very short-lived. In fact, an emotion only lasts about 90 seconds! The reason they often feel longer is because we sustain them with lots of thinking, story-telling, and worry on top of the initial emotion. By pausing to notice the physical sensations and manifestations of the emotion, we offer it a safe "container" in which it can be held, instead of allowing it to overwhelm our experience.

Notice if there's an urge to immediately try to "solve" the emotion. See if you can stay with your physical sensations instead of immediately acting upon them (especially because we are unlikely to act wisely while we are in a heated emotional state). Just stay.

If staying with the sensations of the emotion is too intense, see if you can ground yourself elsewhere in your body—feel your feet on the floor, the temperature of the air on your skin, the sensations in your hands. This reorientation of your attention from the emotion to neutral places in your body can support your mindful pause.

see if you can stay with your physical sensations

Label the emotion

Once you notice a slight settling in your body, see if you can identify the emotion you are experiencing. Psychiatrist and author Dan Siegel calls this practice "Name It to Tame It;" the very act of labeling our emotion allows us a bit of distance from its intensity and invites us to see it more clearly. What felt like anger a moment before may actually be fear; what appeared to be frustration may actually be jealousy. See if you can bring awareness to what this really is.

Identify the unmet need

One of my teachers speaks of identifying "the unmet need that is sponsoring this emotion." Once you've labeled your emotion, can you see if there is an unmet need that triggered it? Perhaps your anger at your husband for not finishing setting up the crib is, in part, sponsored by a need for order and completion. Sensing this need, can you share it with your husband and find a way to meet it?

This way of handling difficult emotions can take a lot of practice, as it requires a sensitivity to your body and a cultivated awareness of how your thoughts and emotions come and go throughout the day. But the more you practice mindfulness (through the specific practices outlined in Chapter 1), the more you will notice a greater attentiveness to your own experience throughout your day. You'll notice emotions as they begin, and you'll be able to name them, explore them, and express the needs beneath them.

This can be a powerful step in being able to advocate for what you need for support—something that is crucial in both pregnancy and motherhood.

Expecting change

While we already know that "things are constantly changing," pregnancy offers us a vivid reminder of this. Your body is changing in ways that are miraculous and frustrating, your relationship with your partner will change as you prepare to become parents, and you've probably already noticed how much your emotions and energy can fluctuate throughout the day. Each day pregnancy offers a reminder that change is the only constant.

And even though we know this, change can still feel unsettling and unmooring. We generally like predictability and stability… and yet motherhood is a time that invites getting comfortable with unpredictability. Research indicates that people who *expect* change, and the occasional stresses that change brings, are more equipped to meet those changes and stresses when they arise. It's when we've convinced ourselves that everything will go according to our plan that even the minor hiccups can feel like major setbacks.

You can begin to practice this with the relatively minor disruptions to your day —traffic jams, late trains, a long line at the checkout. When you notice feelings of irritation, or a sense that "it's not supposed to be this way," perhaps remind yourself,

> *"My day will not unfold entirely as I planned it. I can meet this disruption with patience."*

Soothing holds

During stressful moments, you can soothe yourself through gentle holds and touches. Take both hands and rub them together to generate a little heat, then place them on your cheeks, followed by your forehead and then your closed eyes. Gently massage your ears if that feels supportive.

Another soothing gesture is placing one or both hands over your heart as you take a few deep breaths. You can also give yourself a gentle hug, noticing what it feels like to offer this kind gesture to yourself. (Later in your pregnancy, as your belly gets bigger, lift your arms and elbows up in front of you to do this, wrapping your hands around your shoulder blades).

your physical well-being

Your body changes in ways that are expected, and unexpected, during pregnancy, and needs special care—for your sake just as much as your baby's. Your mindfulness practice can support you in caring for your changing body, and in meeting the challenges that those changes might bring.

Mindfulness of pain

The bodily changes of pregnancy can be exciting, and they can also be painful. (If you are experiencing significant pain, be sure to contact your healthcare provider.) Mindfulness is a powerful strategy for working with pain—in fact, the earliest research on mindfulness in the West came out of clinics using mindfulness to treat patients who suffered from chronic pain. If you are experiencing aches and pains in your body, try the practice opposite.

First, allow your attention to go to the pain itself. (You may not need to even do this step—your attention is likely already there!)

Next, get curious about your pain. "Pain" is just a word; what does this sensation actually feel like? Is it sharp or dull, continuous or intermittent, intense or mild? Is it a tugging, a pinching, a tingling, or something else? (If the sensation is too intense, you don't have to stay on this step.)

Gradually allow your attention to expand out from the center of this sensation. Can you move to the edges of this "pain"? Can you find the place where "pain" becomes "not pain"? Can you expand your attention even further out and into the rest of your body?

As you do this, what is happening to the original pain you felt? For many people, this practice of expanding the attention outward from discomfort often brings a significant shift in their experience of the pain.

You can practice a variation of this any time you experience discomfort or unpleasant sensations. Can you place your attention somewhere else in the body that feels neutral or even pleasant?

Managing thoughts about pain

Research indicates that using mindfulness to manage your pain during pregnancy can support you through labor, too. When you feel pain arising in your body, a helpful practice is to notice it (see previous page) and then investigate what thoughts arise in response to it. For many of us, our response might be a thought like, "This is too intense," "I can't handle this pain," "This pain will never go away," or "What if it gets worse?" Whatever thoughts you notice, just allow them to be there, without judgment.

See if you can notice the thought without engaging it. For example, the thought "What if it gets worse?" might be followed by fear, and then perhaps additional story-telling such as, "I'll never make it through labor if I can't handle this pain." And then, pretty soon, you're wrapped up in an unhelpful thought pattern.

With mindfulness, we practice "uncoupling" the thoughts about our pain from the pain itself. Can you focus on the sensations of the pain and not the thoughts and worries? While this might sound counterintuitive, you might also notice that not getting carried away in the emotional storm makes the pain less intense and more manageable.

If you can practice bringing this type of awareness to the pain and discomfort that you might experience during your pregnancy, it may then be easier to uncouple from the thoughts about pain during labor.

tips

SIGNIFICANT PAIN

If you experience significant pain during your pregnancy, speak to your healthcare provider about finding ways to alleviate it. Please also note that practices that involve noticing pain may feel a bit too intense. You should only bring your attention to your pain if you are able to do so without becoming agitated; bring as much awareness to the sensations as your system allows, and when it's too intense, allow your attention to shift elsewhere, to perhaps a more neutral sensation in the body.

Sleep is the best meditation

Fatigue is a common experience in pregnancy, and you can choose to see it as a wonderful side-effect. Your body needs a lot of rest to support you and nurture your baby. Can you see your tiredness as an invitation from your body to slow down and take care of yourself? Can you reframe exhaustion as the wise knowing of your nervous system telling you to prioritize your well-being? The Dalai Lama once quipped that "sleep is the best meditation." Set an intention to pay attention to your body's signals, and when your body needs to rest, let rest be your practice.

As your pregnancy progresses, you may find sleeping more difficult, due to physical discomfort or other worries. Even if you are unable to sleep, taking the time to physically rest—allowing your body to relax, letting your eyes close so you can briefly pause all the visual information you take in, letting the activity of the mind settle—can be just as nourishing. Even 5–10 minutes of rest can do wonders.

nourish yourself with rest

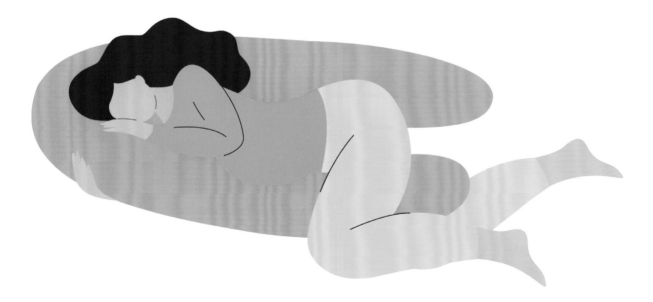

Massage

If you are able to, you may want to schedule a prenatal massage with a trained masseuse who specializes in pregnancy treatments and can help address specific discomforts or alleviate tension. Check with your healthcare provider about their recommendations for massage during pregnancy; many advise waiting until the second trimester. It's also recommended to use light, broad strokes instead of deep tissue massage during pregnancy.

If you don't have that option, you could ask your partner to give you a massage. Lie on your side, with a pillow between your knees if that feels supportive. Your partner could massage your neck, shoulders, and upper back, and gently use their fist to massage your lower back (on either side of the spine, not directly on it) to alleviate lower back pain. A gentle massage on the scalp, arms, and legs can also be soothing.

Mindful eating

With all the advice about what to eat, and not to eat, during pregnancy, sometimes mealtimes can provoke anxiety or be seen as a chore. Give yourself a bit of extra time (if possible!) to eat a meal slowly and mindfully. Take a moment to see and smell the food before you eat, offering gratitude to all the people who made your meal possible (especially if that includes you!). After taking a bite, place your fork back down and truly taste your food as you bring your full attention to the act of eating. What is it like not to rush into scooping up the next bite? What tastes and sensations do you notice? Allow yourself a few moments to eat, and savor, your food in silence. (See also page 75.) This act of nourishing yourself is a true act of self-care.

self-care

Self-care is critical for mothers; we cannot care for others if we do not resource ourselves. If you don't have a self-care routine, pregnancy is a great time to discover the activities that nourish you, ones that you can continue to do in your own home in the midst of mothering.

think of simple practices you can do just where you are, in any moment

Self-care menu

We often think of self-care as spa days and pedicures, but those are usually not a sustainable plan. I encourage you to develop a Self-care Menu, with a list of the practices that you find nurturing. Think of activities that bring you a sense of joy, rest, fulfillment, contentment, or ease. While self-care is highly personal, I'd like to suggest several activities that you may find supportive:

- Sitting down to have a warm cup of decaf tea or coffee (or if you're feeling hot, a nice cold drink)
- Allowing yourself a few moments to sit or lie down and close your eyes
- Giving yourself a gentle hand massage with a favorite lotion
- Taking a moment to chat with your partner, or call or text a friend
- Doing something creative—coloring, drawing, painting, writing, sewing
- Listening (and singing along to) your favorite music
- Taking a quick nap
- Writing in a journal
- Snuggling under a warm blanket
- Sitting outside for a few moments and watching the clouds, birds, etc.
- Lighting a scented candle and just sitting for a few minutes
- Taking a walk around the block
- Reading a poem (try Rumi or Mary Oliver)
- Doing a jigsaw or crossword puzzle

While self-care activities can be varied, I encourage you to think of simple practices that you can do just where you are, in (almost) any moment. These practices will be very supportive for the times when you are at home with your newborn and need of a bit of self-nurturing.

chapter 3

CREATING A
Special
BOND

MINDFUL MOMENTS WITH YOUR UNBORN BABY

If it's ever felt strange to you when someone asks if you're excited to "meet" your baby, or to bring him home, it's probably because you are already deeply in relationship with him. He's been living with you for weeks or months already, connecting with your daily rhythms of movement and rest. As your pregnancy progresses, he'll attune to your voice, and you'll begin to learn his daily rhythms, too. You are creating a special bond; you are connected physically, not only through the umbilical cord, but through the resonance of your nervous systems. And this physical connection can support you in cultivating a deep emotional relationship to your baby long before he is born. The practices in this chapter will support you in connecting to your body and your baby's body as you begin creating this visceral and emotional bond.

meditation with your baby

These short meditations, both formal and informal, allow you to focus on your baby and your growing bond.

Baby bump meditation

Place your hands on your belly and take a few deep breaths. Notice how this short moment of connection to your baby feels. Throughout your day, you probably instinctively or protectively place your hands on your belly; see if you can bring attention to the times you do this, and make it a mindful moment of connection with your baby, taking deep, relaxing breaths.

Belly breathing for two

Place your hands on your belly, allow your eyes to close, and take a few deep breaths. With each in-breath, imagine all the nourishing oxygen and nutrients you are bringing into your body and sharing with your baby. With each out-breath, allow your body to relax a bit more deeply, and imagine your baby relaxing with you. Visualize the movement of your belly with each breath as a gentle way of rocking and soothing your baby. Continue focusing on your breath, with each in-breath representing a taking in of all that you and your baby need, and each out-breath representing a letting go, a release of any tension or worry that you don't need.

visualize the movement of your belly with each breath as a gentle way of rocking and soothing your baby

Lovingkindness for your baby

Lovingkindness is a powerful mindfulness practice in which we send kind and loving wishes to another person. For this practice, take a moment to think about what you *most* want for your child. While you likely have lots of dreams and hopes for your baby, consider the things that are most essential—how do you want your child to feel, to love, to be?

You can use the phrases in the practice below if they are helpful, or you can add kind wishes or dreams of your own.

Take a few deep breaths, place your hand on your heart, and, envisioning your baby, say quietly to yourself:

"May you be healthy…"

"May you be happy…"

"May you be safe…"

"May you be loved, and loving…"

"May you be strong…"

"May you know kindness and joy."

Notice how it feels to send these kind wishes to your baby. You may find it helpful to journal about this practice, or even write a letter to your baby, expressing your heartfelt wishes and dreams for his amazing life ahead.

Heartbeat meditation

Sit or lie down in a comfortable position, and take a moment to find your pulse, perhaps on your wrist or neck. Bring your attention to the sensation of your pulse, knowing that with each beat of your heart, your body is sending oxygen and nutrients and a whole bunch of love to your baby. You may want to take just a few deep breaths and reflect on the absolute miracle of this process, the way your body knows exactly how to care for your little one… and the fact that you are literally growing a human deep in your belly! If you find it supportive, you could also incorporate lovingkindness phrases for your baby into this practice (see opposite).

If you are far along enough into your pregnancy to be able to hear your baby's heartbeat with a stethoscope or a monitor, you could shift your attention to the sound of her heartbeat. Notice how much faster her tiny heart beats compared to yours; already, your bodies are deeply connected, interdependent and yet unique. Notice the sensations, emotions, thoughts, wishes, and everything else that arises as you listen to your baby's heartbeat.

Involve your partner

As your baby grows in your belly, it's natural for your partner to feel a bit "left out" of the experience. See if you can involve your partner in the practices in this chapter; for example, having them place their hands on your belly, noting how it moves as you breathe, and also noticing the baby's movements. Toward the end of your pregnancy, your baby can hear sounds and voices from outside your body, so encourage your partner to talk or sing to your bump.

you and your bump

While you cannot see your baby during pregnancy (ultrasound scans aside), this section offers way to connect with her while she is still happily residing in your tummy.

Mindful movement

One of the greatest joys of pregnancy is feeling your baby move in your belly. At first, these movements are tiny flutters, progressing to more energetic kicks, and eventually they become undulating waves of activity that others can easily see. When you notice your baby moving, place your hand where you felt the movement. And just pause. Notice if you immediately want to tell your partner about the baby's activity, or if you want someone else to feel her movement. While it's a joy to share your baby's kicks and punches, see if you can let this particular movement be just for you. What do you envision she's doing in there? What does it actually feel like as she wriggles in your belly? Are her movements slow or fast, forceful or gentle, continuous or intermittent? Just notice all you can; savor this experience of another life growing and moving inside you.

see if you can let this particular movement be just for you

Mindful ultrasounds

The interesting thing about all the technology that allows us to know so much about your baby before he is born is that it can have the unintended effect of distancing you from him. When your baby's image is projected onto the ultrasound screen, your eyes and your attention are taken away from your body. Your baby appears separate from you, black-and-white and fuzzy on a small digital screen. When you have your ultrasounds during your pregnancy, see if you can try to keep a little bit of your attention on your body—and your baby in your belly. It is certainly thrilling to get that image of what your baby looks like, so enjoy all the excitement of the moment, but see if a small part of your focus can remain internal, on that little baby that you already know so well inside you.

Mindful eating for two

Each time you eat, you are now not only nourishing yourself, but your baby as well. Once in a while, you might try eating your meal, or even just drinking a glass of water, slowly and mindfully, considering how you are nurturing your baby and savoring the moment. Even the most simple acts that you engage in throughout your day are now, in a very real way, a gesture of motherly love.

tips

EATING MINDFULLY

If you feel you do not know how to begin eating mindfully, follow these tips:

- Place your fork down between each bite as you eat. Notice if your normal tendency is to start scooping up your next bite before you've even finished chewing this one!
- See if you can really pay attention to the sensations of eating: the smell and texture of the food, the movement of your mouth and body, and of course, the taste.

getting prepared

There can be much to do to get ready for your baby's entrance into the world, and you can make readying yourself and your home a part of your mindfulness practice.

Setting up the nursery

Setting up and decorating a nursery for your baby can be incredibly joyful and exciting, and it can also be a lot of hard work. What would it be like to approach it as a mindfulness practice? Can you bring your full attention to folding the newborn baby clothes you have bought? To hanging a picture on the wall? To building the crib?

This practice of bringing your attention to a household task, like changing sheets or putting away laundry, is a powerful way of infusing your day with presence. It really is about noticing what it's like to engage in each task you are doing as you

are doing it: noticing the scent of the laundry or the soft feel of the sheets; noticing all the movements of your body as you organize drawers and hang decorations.

This doesn't mean, necessarily, that you have to like engaging in these tasks or that you must bring an inauthentic level of enthusiasm to them. It simply means you do them with your full attention, so that the act of folding laundry or organizing the bookshelf becomes a meditation in and of itself. Your task is your anchor in this practice, the way your breath is perhaps the focus of your regular meditation practice. How can you infuse dignity and intention in these tasks that are often done when you're distracted, or your mind is somewhere else?

If it's supportive to you, you could extend this practice by imagining your baby in the room, wearing these clothes or playing with these books. Make each part of setting up the nursery a part of your practice and another way to bond with your baby.

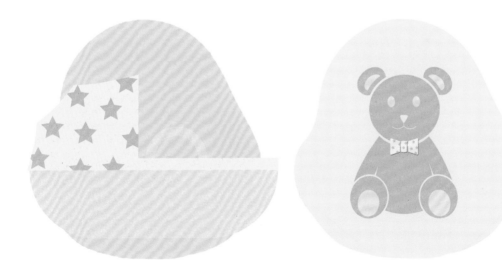

Beginner's mind

In mindfulness practice we speak of having a "beginner's mind," approaching the world as if everything were new and unfamiliar. And that is exactly how your baby will meet the world in a few months! See if, for a few moments each day, you can approach whatever you're doing with a beginner's mind. How would someone who's never washed dishes before, for example, approach the task? What would they notice?

Look around your home and notice the shapes and colors and textures that will soon fascinate your baby. What are you excited to show him? Look at the nursery you've set up and see it through your child's eyes. As you walk through your neighborhood, imagine you are your baby seeing it for the first time. Try working through the practice below.

Not only does this practice help you cultivate your own ability to pay greater attention to the world around you, but it supports you in developing empathy for your child in seeing the world the way he may encounter it.

Take a few deep breaths, and let your gaze just take in your surroundings.

Can you notice three things in this space that you haven't really noticed before, or haven't attended to in a while?

Can you identify three different sounds that you're hearing right now? See if you can just notice the actual qualities of the sounds, instead of just noticing that you can hear a "car" or "birds."

What does it feel like to take in your everyday surroundings in this more mindful way?

Baby talk

By the early part of your third trimester, your baby is able to hear your voice, as well as sounds from outside your body. Spend some time each day talking to your baby—you could repeat the lovingkindness wishes (see page 70), or you could simply narrate what you are doing. For example, as you are tidying up the house or driving to work, you could tell your baby about your day or about the activities you are doing. Not only is this a helpful way for *you* to be mindful, by paying attention to your present-moment experience, but it's also a great way to start sharing your experience with your baby and introducing her to the rhythms of your day and the cadence of your voice.

Read to your baby

As you start building your baby's library of books, spend a few moments each night reading a book to your bump. Your baby will start to become familiar with the sound of your voice, and you'll get to discover your favorite bedtime stories to share with him after he's born.

Mindful journaling

Journaling is a powerful practice to support your own reflection and growth, and journaling your pregnancy can be a special way to bond with your baby (and it could be a fun gift to share with her when she's older!). It could be combined with your gratitude journal (see page 65). You could include photos of your growing bump, as well as your thoughts and dreams about your baby. Use these pages to make a start.

chapter 4

HAVING A

Mindful

LABOR AND BIRTH

PRACTICES TO SUPPORT YOU IN EACH STAGE OF LABOR

You are probably getting lots of solicited and unsolicited advice about labor and childbirth. And while I'll be sharing some suggestions with you in this chapter, ultimately the way you birth your baby comes down to choices you will make for *you*, in consultation with your healthcare provider and your partner.

There are many ways that mindfulness can support you in labor, from relaxation and pain-management techniques to the general way in which you can approach your birth plan and the birthing experience. In many ways, birth is a perfect lesson in how our motherhood journey will unfold in unexpected ways; with mindfulness, you can meet the process with presence and intention.

the best-laid birth plans...

You've probably been spending a lot of time envisioning your baby's birth... and your healthcare provider has probably encouraged you to develop your birth plan, where you describe your preferences for how you would like your labor and delivery to be managed. It's helpful to bring your mindfulness practice to the process of creating your birth plan. One thing mindfulness teaches us is that things rarely go according to our plan; life has its own way of unfolding (see page 39)! Labor can take a few hours or a few days, you may deliver vaginally or by C-section; each birth presents in its own way. Assuming you are working with your provider and are informed by medical guidelines, there is no right or wrong way to labor and to bring your baby into the world.

While it's important to consider your wishes and goals for your baby's birth, and to communicate them to your healthcare team, it's also worth approaching your "birth plan" as "birth intentions." There are so many unknowns in this process, and the more tightly you cling to a particular vision of how it will be, the more likely it is that you'll get frustrated when things don't unfold in the manner you envisioned.

Considering your birth intentions

Give yourself some time for the practice (overleaf). Allow yourself space to get comfortable, perhaps have a soothing warm tea or play some gentle music in the background, and have a journal and pen to hand. You may choose to record the practice so that you can listen to it with your eyes closed.

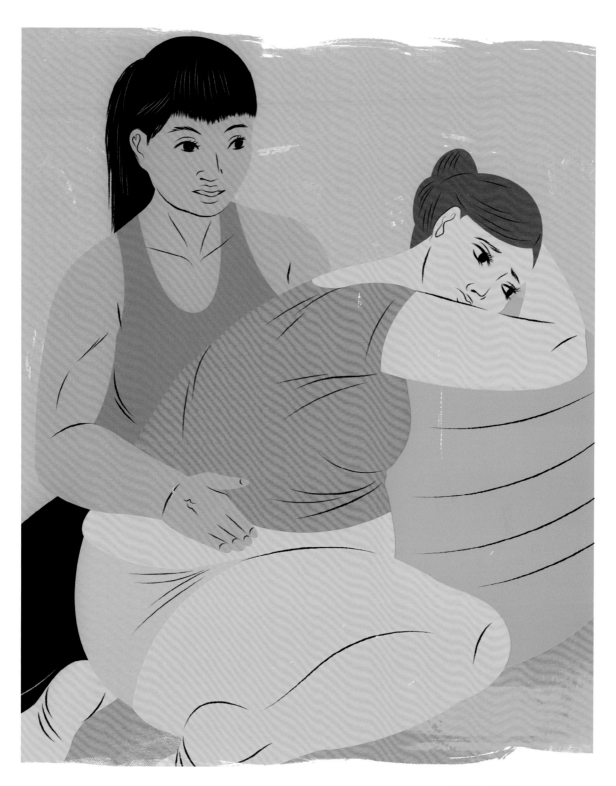

Close your eyes and allow yourself to envision, with just the lightest touch of detail, your baby's labor and delivery.

If you've already chosen the hospital or location where you will birth, imagine yourself in that setting. See yourself entering the room, still in the early stages of labor and fully able to take in your surroundings. How does the room feel? Is it light or dark? Is there music playing? What is in the room? Are there blankets, pillows, or other comfort items? How do you feel in this room? Relaxed, excited, nervous, or something else? Consider if there is anything you would like to change about the room to support you in feeling the way you want to feel…

Spend some time just visualizing yourself in this room, and notice what images come to mind or what sensations you notice. Make a mental note of the things that make you feel comfortable and soothed, and perhaps even pause this practice for a moment to write down in your journal the ideas that arise for you. What feels supportive in this space? Truly, how do you want to feel as you labor?

As gently as possible, imagine yourself as your labor begins to progress, as your contractions start to become more frequent and intense. Consider, as best you can, how you want to feel through this process. Would it make you feel more comfortable to alleviate your pain through medication or an epidural? Would it make you feel more comfortable not to use medication? It's okay if you aren't sure right now… just spend some time considering how these questions land for you. There's no right or wrong way to answer them—this is about discovering what really matters to you in this process.

As you imagine your labor continuing to progress, visualize who is present in the room with you. If your partner is there, how is he or she supporting you? What would make you feel safe and comfortable? Do you want your mother, a dear friend, or someone else there? How do you envision them supporting you?

As you continue, try to envision **how** you will labor. Are you lying down? Have you been walking? Do you think it would be supportive to take a bath or a shower? Are you using a birthing ball? Can you visualize laboring in a birth pool? Again, you don't need to make all these decisions right now; just notice how these suggestions feel as you even consider them.

Return to the question of how you want to **feel** as you labor, both physically and emotionally. Is there anything else we haven't considered that would help you feel that way?

Take a few deep breaths, and spend some time journaling about what you noticed as you explored some of your birthing options.

Note your reactions

Your healthcare provider will likely discuss many of your birth plan options during your prenatal visits. As these conversations occur, notice what happens in your body as certain options are mentioned. Do some cause a tightening or a contraction (of your general body, not a labor contraction!)? Do some create a sense of relaxation, looseness, or ease in the body? Take notice of the signals your body sends you as you consider how you'd like to labor.

You don't need to be a warrior

As you consider how you wish to birth your baby, you're likely hearing advice from all sides about whether you will make use of pain-relieving medications or procedures. You already know this, but I'll gently remind you: this decision is yours to make.

finding comfort

Throughout your labor and birth, it will be helpful to find ways to increase your physical comfort and aid you in feeling relaxed and calm. Spend some time now exploring what those might be for you—perhaps gentle movement or rocking, massage (see page 60), heat or coolness, visualization, mantras, a focal object, breathing techniques, or listening to music.

Mantras

You may find mantras helpful during labor. You can think of a mantra as an inspiring or reassuring phrase that helps you relax or sustain your energy. I encourage you to think of words or quotes that are meaningful to you, or you may consider one of the following phrases:

> *"My body knows how to do this."*

> *"I have all that I need."*

> *"This is hard, but I can do hard things."*

> *"This is a miraculous moment."*

> *"My body is amazing and powerful."*

You may choose to write down your mantra on a piece of paper so that you can pin it up on the wall where you will be birthing. It might even be a soothing activity to spend some time decorating it and adding supportive or encouraging images.

Visualization

You can use your mindfulness practice in the months before your birth to explore what a safe, soothing place looks like for you, visualizing it and creating as much detail in your mind as you can. You then have the option of imagining being there during labor.

You could spend a few moments each day taking a few deep breaths and imagining relaxing there; the more you bring your mind back to this special place, the more easily you will be able to access these mental images and comforting sensations while you are laboring. You may choose to record the following practice so that you can listen to it with your eyes closed.

Close your eyes and think of a place where you feel completely safe and relaxed. This could be somewhere in your home, such as your bedroom, or a favorite beach, park, or other relaxing environment. You could also imagine an ideal safe and soothing place that would make you feel comfortable and at ease.

As you envision this place in your mind, take a moment to really "see" it. What is here? This is your comfort space, so you can fill it with anything that would soothe you: soft blankets, warm sunshine, a cup of tea, bright flowers, a trusted friend. Spend some time "decorating" this space in your mind, making it your personal sanctuary.

Explore what it might feel like to be there. How does your body feel? Can you imagine any tension being released? Can you feel a sense of ease in your body as you let the muscles of your legs, arms, neck, and face relax? Imagine all the tightness draining from your body. Release any unnecessary holding or tension. Can you picture yourself here, in a bed or on the beach or somewhere in this space where you can allow yourself to fully let go?

Are there soothing sounds in this place, such as your favorite music, the waves of the ocean, the singing of birds, or the gentle sounds of a river stream? Are there comforting scents, such as your favorite oils or the smell of the sea, flowers, soft grass, or something else?

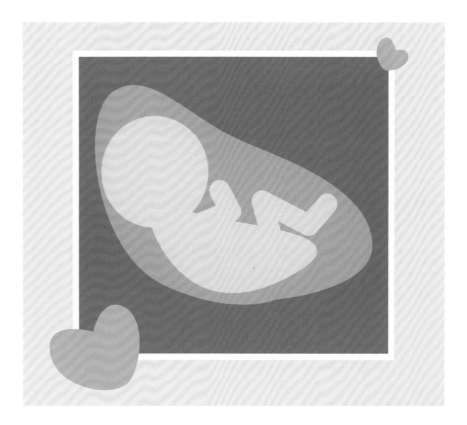

Focal object

Is there a meaningful object you could have with you as you labor to focus your attention on? This object could be a photograph of your own mother, or an ultrasound picture of your baby. It could be a favorite flower, a meaningful artwork, a note or card from a loved one, or a piece of clothing you've purchased for your baby.

You can bring whatever you've chosen into the birthing room, and any time you experience physical or emotional overwhelm during your labor, bring your attention to this object. When you do, try to *really see* it: what color is it, what shape is it, why is it special to you? Gently shifting your attention to something other than your discomfort can provide some momentary relief.

Music

Create a labor playlist of music that you find soothing and comforting. If you'd like, you could play the music in the background as you do your mindfulness practice, while taking a few deep breaths, or while lying down to rest or nap. This can help you associate the music with being relaxed and at ease, which will support you as you labor.

tip
MINDFUL REMINDER

As you plan for your labor, keep in mind that the comfort items and practices you have chosen may not actually be soothing or what you need in any given moment as you birth. As with your birth plan, try not to not hold too tightly to any particular vision of how your baby's birth will unfold. A powerful part of mindfulness practice is being flexible and adjusting to what is true in the moment.

Progressive relaxation

In the earlier stages of labor, you may find progressive relaxation exercises to be helpful; they can allow you to get some much-needed rest as you prepare for more active labor. As the name implies, progressive relaxation consists of relaxing each part of your body in turn.

To do this, you may find it helpful for your partner or other attendant to read the phrases below to you.

Take a breath in, and tighten the muscles in both feet. Scrunch your toes and notice the sensations of tightness, and then as you breathe out, relax your feet. Notice the changes in the sensations in your feet as you do this. Do you notice tingling, or heat, or a feeling of expansion? Keeping your feet relaxed, take another breath in and out as you become aware of what it feels like to release tension and allow your feet to rest.

On the next breath in, tense the muscles of your legs, again noticing what it feels like, and then relax the muscles in your legs as you breathe out. Imagine giving all the weight of your legs to the bed, chair, or whatever is supporting you. What does it feel like to fully let go?

You can repeat this progressive relaxation in its entirety, or return to tensing and releasing specific parts of your body. Practicing this earlier in your pregnancy will be helpful as you learn the exercises that are most supportive for you.

You may find that sometimes it is quite difficult to relax, or to release tension in a particular area of your body. That's okay! If that happens, try placing your attention somewhere in your body that feels relaxed or pleasant instead.

On the next in-breath, tense your hands and see what you notice, and then breathe out and let your hands relax. What does it feel like to let your hands be loose and fully at rest?

On the next in-breath, tighten the muscles in your arms, and then breathe out as you let them release. Notice the sensations in your arms, or anywhere else in your body, as you sink further into relaxation.

On the next breath in, scrunch up the muscles of your face (or do this without coordinating with the breath if that's easier), and then release those muscles as you exhale. What does it feel like to let all the muscles of your face—your jaw, your eyes, your brow—be at ease?

trust your body

As you continue to practice the body scan exercise (see pages 30–31) as part of your mindfulness practice, you'll become more familiar with the sensations of and signals from your body. This will be incredibly supportive while you are in labor, as birth is (obviously) a very physical and sensory experience. The more in tune you are with your body, aware of various muscle contractions or changes in your breath, the more you can move with its natural rhythms and processes.

Labor positions

We often see women in movies giving birth while lying on their backs (and certainly this position can work, and is a necessity if you have an epidural). But there are many different positions in which you can labor. Attuning to the sensations of your body will be very helpful—you may notice an urge to stand, or to squat, or to position yourself on all-fours, for example. Listen to the signals of your body as you labor; it knows what to do.

Breathing exercises

You may likely learn a variety of breathing techniques in your birthing preparation classes, and your midwife or doctor may also suggest specific breath patterns during labor. Before your birth, take some time to experiment with the breathing practices below, noting which ones help you feel comfort and ease.

Counting your breath

Count from one to ten with your breath, breathing in "one," breathing out "two," breathing in "three," breathing out "four," and so on. If you are interrupted or distracted or lose count, or reach ten, start over again at one.

In through the nose, out through the mouth

Many women find this a supportive breathing practice through labor. Take a deep breath in through your nose, and then open your mouth as you exhale. Depending on the intensity of your labor, you can let your out-breath be a gentle sigh, or a more vocal and audible exhale.

Relax around the pain

It is a natural instinct to tighten around pain as you experience it. (Think of how your body tenses when you are hurt, or how your attention is so quickly drawn to a headache or other body pain.) As the sensations are so unfamiliar and can be quite intense, the discomfort of childbirth can trigger a similar tightening in your body. This tensing, while an understandable reaction to something that is unpleasant, can actually intensify the pain—you might be literally contracting around your contraction!

To support you in relaxing around the pain, you can return to your breath. During intense labor discomfort, it may be helpful to bring your attention to the breath in the nose, as it will direct your attention away from your abdomen. See if you can feel each breath come in through the nose, and then exhale (perhaps loudly!) through the mouth.

Befriend the pain

Research indicates that women who perceive pain during labor as normal, and even helpful, have more empowering birth experiences. In almost every other area of our life, pain is usually a signal that something is "wrong," and is assumed to be "bad" (again, you can blame evolution for that one!) But during labor, the pain is, for the most part, a normal and helpful part of the process. The pain during a contraction is a sign that your body is doing exactly what it was designed to do as the uterus contracts to prepare your body, and your baby, for delivery. It's the painful sensations that trigger the urge in your body to push during the final stages of labor. It may help to think of some supportive mantras or phrases now that could help you during labor, such as:

"This pain is helping me."

"I can handle this pain."

*"I will work **with** this pain, and not against it."*

your body is doing exactly what it was designed to do

Savor the rest

Contrary to the way labor is often portrayed on TV or in the movies, it is not a constant stream of pain and yelling. In between the contractions are periods of rest. The rest is a powerful reminder that every contraction comes to an end. If you can, in the midst of a contraction, remind yourself that this pain is temporary, and a period of rest will follow. This is a powerful place to practice "uncoupling" your thoughts about the pain from the pain itself (see Chapter 2). Notice if you're thinking, "I can't handle this" or "What if the next one is worse?" Befriend the pain (as best you can), know that the rest will always follow, and savor it when it arrives.

A labor of love

As labor progresses and becomes more intense, can you focus on your love for your baby and how excited you are to meet him or her? As clichéd as the phrase is, this is a labor of love, and this love can help sustain you through the final stages. You may even want to have a special mantra to support you, such as:

"I do this for love."

"I do this for [your baby's name, if you've chosen one]."

chapter 5

Mindful

MOTHERHOOD

NAVIGATING THE FIRST FEW WEEKS WITH YOUR BABY

Your mindfulness practice will be incredibly supportive to you in the weeks and months (and years!) ahead. Your baby will enter this world primed to bond with you, and the primary way you will do this is through carefully attuning to her signals. The mindfulness practices in this chapter will help to support the deep attachment and relationship you have with your baby.

early days

The first three months of your baby's life is seen as the "fourth trimester," as it is a crucial period of development during which she adjusts to life outside your belly, and for you as you get to know her and adjust to the rhythms of motherhood. For both of you, this is a period of great transition as your bodies and brains change. In many ways, living with a newborn is about learning to be at peace with constant change, and with being out of control—a skill that is crucial for the entire motherhood journey.

Mama and baby meditation

In those first early weeks, you could do your formal mindfulness practice with your baby while he sleeps. As you hold him, notice his breath and heart rate in relation to yours. If your breath begins to slow down, does his? If your heart rate slows down, does his? You've spent several months together syncing your bodily rhythms, and you may notice the calming effect your nervous system has on him.

Moments of presence

One of the most powerful things my mindfulness teachers
at Mindful Schools taught me was that I didn't have to be
mindful 100% of the time (it's pretty much impossible!). They
emphasized, instead, brief moments of awareness, repeated
many times. In these first few weeks at home with your baby,
you'll likely have many moments of distraction, sleepiness, and
forgetfulness. It's part of the adjustment to these very early
stages of motherhood. So please go easy on yourself when
distraction seems more common than presence.

But when presence arises—maybe when you see one of
your baby's "practice smiles" flash on her face while she sleeps,
or as you watch your partner or your older children speak
"baby-talk" to her—simply be present. Savor those brief
moments of awareness and presence.

Feeding time

When my children were infants, I remember hearing the advice that I should never have the TV on or be distracted when I was nursing or feeding them; I should use that time to gaze lovingly at them and bond with them.

Confession: I sometimes watched 90s sitcom re-runs while nursing my babies. Sometimes I just needed a break. And it was beautiful.

And sometimes, I did stare in amazement at their tiny heads, their skinny fingers resting on my chest, and their contented, sleepy faces when they were done nursing. And it was beautiful.

My advice: when you need feeding time just to be about your need to sit and watch a show because the day's been crazy and hectic, then let it just be about you taking time for you. And when you feel resourced, let feeding time be about staring in amazement at your amazing baby.

let feeding time be
whatever you need
it to be

Soften

Nursing mothers often experience upper back and shoulder pain, especially if they're in a hunched-over posture as they nurse. Mothers who are bottle-feeding may suffer from the same problem.

Each time you begin to feed your baby, remind yourself to "soften": relax your shoulders and allow your head to rest gently on your spine, instead of craning forward. See if you can release tension anywhere else in your body. Using supportive pillows under your arms, beneath your baby, and/or behind your back can help to get you into a position where you are not straining to hold yourself in place.

You'll probably notice in these early days that the release of progesterone while nursing makes you quite sleepy; this can sometimes help you relax, or it may cause a more hunched posture. See if you can adjust your position so you remain comfortable while you nurse; the more relaxed you are, the more easily your baby can relax.

You may also find it supportive to do some "chest openers"—while standing or seated, bring your arms out to the side. Bend them at the elbows so that your arms are in a "goalpost" pose. Then gently bring your shoulder blades together as your arms move backward, and your chest naturally pushes forward and opens a bit. Be gentle as you move, and notice the sensations in your back, chest, and neck as you stretch. Repeat this a few times each day during the weeks or months that you are nursing.

BOTTLES

If you are bottle-feeding, you can use special bottles to support a healthy posture while feeding. They are bent to encourage semi-upright feeding, which can help reduce digestion issues for your baby and enable you to sit in a more comfortable position, too.

Soothing

As you've probably figured out, your baby has an immature nervous system, and is unable to self-regulate or calm himself down. Another key way to support your baby during the fourth trimester is by acting as his external nervous system. When he is unable to soothe himself, he needs you to help. The primary ways you do this are through your voice and your touch. Holding your baby and breathing deeply, or gently rocking him, are powerful, almost instinctive ways in which you teach his nervous system to enter states of regulation and calm.

Your baby has been able to hear your voice through most of the third trimester, so he is already distinctly attuned to the prosody and cadence of your speech. Singing lullabies, gently narrating your day, and speaking in a slightly higher-pitched voice (often called "motherese") can all help to soothe your baby and help the two of you bond.

Wear your baby

Since your touch and physical presence is so important to soothing your baby, try to "wear" your baby with a sling as much as you are able. When she was in your belly, she was used to being rocked to sleep as you walked, and she's already familiar with the patterns of your day. (Wearing a sling can also give your arms and upper back a break from carrying her.) This doesn't mean you need to be attached all day long, but it can help to comfort and soothe her when needed.

Mindful listening

Part of the fourth trimester is you and your baby learning to pick up on each other's signals. She will begin to learn certain patterns in your voice that indicate safety, comfort, or joy. And you may start to notice slight variations in her vocalizations that indicate if she is sleepy, wet, hungry, or overstimulated. It can take a while to learn your child's patterns (and, I confess, I never quite got the hang of it!) so be patient, and certainly be forgiving with yourself if all her cries sound the same to you.

I offer this practice of mindful listening because the cries from your baby may be intense or startling, or may feel all-too-frequent, and by placing your attention on the particular details of the cries (rather than on the panicked sensations her cries may elicit in you), you may not feel so jolted or unsettled by them.

Sleep when the baby sleeps

Okay, I know you've heard this one a hundred times already… but that's because it's important. You may be tempted to clean the house or scroll on your phone when you finally get your baby to sleep, but you need your rest, too. It will likely be some time before you get a full night's sleep, so napping, or even just resting, frequently is essential. This is your first step in fully resourcing yourself so that you can be there for your baby; self-care (including naps) is a must for mothers!

be patient and forgiving with yourself

Let your world be small

In the first few days after my daughter's birth, as I stayed in the hospital recovering from my C-section, I was struck by how beautifully small my world had become. I was on maternity leave, so there were no distractions from work. Meals were brought to me on a predictable schedule. My husband stayed overnight on the quite uncomfortable-looking lounge chair in my hospital room that for three days was my entire world. All I had to focus on was my daughter… and our newly created family. Once we returned home, we did our best to keep our world small—a few visitors here and there, a few meals delivered— but for the most part, I enjoyed being in a protective cocoon of simply caring for my daughter. As the days and weeks progressed, and I healed from surgery, I was able to take on a bit more responsibility. And I looked back with longing on those not-easy-but-simple days when my world was so small.

So if you can, let your world be small. Let the emails and laundry and other tasks wait. They will be there when you're ready for them. In these first few weeks, accept the offers of help that will support you in these moments of just being with your baby.

If you notice any self-judgment for "letting things slide," remind yourself that this is a brief period of your, and your baby's, life—give yourself full permission to allow life to be simple and small.

If you have other children at home, see if it's possible to have a family member or even an older child from your neighborhood spend a few hours with them so that you can spend simple, quiet time with your baby.

This, too, shall pass

My own mother says this all the time, and it was probably most meaningful to me in those early days at home with my babies, when I felt I was in a fog of sleep-deprivation and childbirth recovery… and often felt unsure of what I was doing. These early days can be hard. They can be amazing. They can be overwhelming. They are full of snuggles and spit up, gentle sighs and messy diapers, loving visitors and sleepless nights. But one day, your baby will sleep through the night, he will be potty trained, and your house will stay relatively tidy. If it's hard right now, that's okay. This, too, shall pass.

appreciating your baby

Although the days can seem long—perhaps endless—in these first few weeks, it truly is a brief time in your baby's life. If you notice yourself wishing the time away (a very normal thought!), see if you can take a mindful moment to create memories to savor.

That baby smell!

Please forgive me for saying that one day you will miss that sweet baby smell! As you hold your baby, see if you can be aware of the full sensory experience of snuggling. Notice the feel of your baby's soft skin, the smell of her head or her breath, the sounds of her coos and sighs, and the movements of her lips and hands and feet. Notice the sensations in your own body as you kiss her feet and fingers and tummy. Allow yourself to be fully in your body and your own sensory experience as you hold her.

Mindful photos

You're probably filling up your phone camera with pictures of your baby. See if each day, you can save just one photo of your baby's face to a special folder; within just a few weeks, you'll be able to marvel over how quickly he's growing and changing.

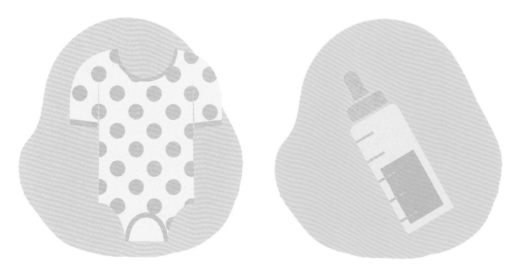

Gratitude journal

Each day, write down one thing that you are thankful for about your baby, or that amazed you about her. And if you don't have time to write it down, simply take a deep breath and call it to mind at the end of the day. And if it's been a super rough day and you can't think of anything (we've ALL had those days!), then simply name one thing you're thankful for (you managed to take a shower, or that it's time for bed), and let yourself rest.

activities with your baby

When your baby is so small, it may feel like he simply sleeps and feeds. But with a little mindful awareness, you'll notice all the ways your baby is developing and how you can introduce him to the world around him.

Spend time outside with your baby

In Chapter 2, I encouraged you to spend time outside to cultivate your sense of awe. If the weather permits, spend time outside with your baby. Spread out a blanket on the grass, and lie down together staring up at the sky. Your baby's reactions to the sensations and smells and sights of the outdoors is likely to spark a renewed sense of joy and awe in you.

tip
SENSORY ACTIVITIES

When it's too cold or wet outdoors, practice the same activity indoors with other sensory stimuli. Move different textures and fabrics over your baby's body, shine lights on the ceiling above him, let your hands dance just in front of him, or gently shake a rattle for him to listen to.

Notice the world for your baby

Though your baby cannot understand the words you say, he is deeply attuned to the sound of your voice, and by learning the cadence and rhythm of your words, he is learning the basics of language. As much as you can, talk to your baby about the world around him—this is a mindfulness practice for both of you! You can describe the colors and textures of his clothes as you dress him, the patterns on his blanket, the sights you see as you go for a walk, or the pictures and furniture in the room where you're sitting. Approach everything with your beginner's mind (see page 78) and see, and describe, your baby's world.

Mirror mirror

An important part of your baby's psychosocial development in the first few months of her life is understanding that her experiences are known by another and mirrored back to her. (This is similar to our adult need to have our experiences understood by others.) The following are ways you can mirror your baby. With your baby in her bouncy seat or in your lap, make eye contact with her. When she blinks her eyes, you blink your eyes. If she yawns, you yawn. In this playful mirroring, you are already teaching her about empathy, and she (in her own baby way) is learning to trust that you are attuned to her experience and can communicate that to her.

As she starts to coo and babble, you can respond by imitating her sounds, or with normal speech. Even though babies speak gibberish, they are learning the give-and-take of conversation. You may have no idea what your baby is actually trying to communicate, and that's okay! The point is to have a "conversation," for example:

"I wonder what we should have for dinner."

Pause.

"Ah, that's a great idea. I'm not sure we have enough eggs, though."

Pause.

"Yes, you're right, we DO have enough eggs to make chicken parmesan! Let's do that."

Be as playful and fun as you can with this. It's a powerful way to bond with your baby and support her growing trust in you.

Baby massage

Massaging your baby is a special way to bond with him, and it's even believed to promote less fussiness and better sleep. It certainly can help your baby relax.

Massage your baby when he's alert, and when it's been at least 45 minutes since his last feed, as you don't want to upset his tummy. Undress your baby, but have a blanket to cover him so he doesn't get cold. You can use a gentle baby lotion but your bare hands are fine, too.

There are several baby massage instruction videos online, but in general you want to use a light touch. Start by gently massaging his scalp and ears, and work downwards to his toes. You could sing to your baby or explain to him what you're doing as you massage him. This can be a sweet way to connect, soothe your baby, and familiarize yourself with his body and how he likes to be comforted.

Reading to your baby

It's never too early to start cultivating a love of books and reading with your baby. Find books that have pictures of faces (which babies love to stare at) and, even though your baby will have no idea what you're saying, talk to him about the pictures, describing what the faces look like and what emotions they are displaying. Read simple stories with colorful artwork, and point out the different colors and shapes to your baby. Reading stories with rhymes or playful use of language is also a great way to help your baby learn to recognize the cadence of speech and the give-and-take of conversation.

Learn mindfulness from your baby

Years ago, a reader landed on my blog after googling "how to teach mindfulness to an infant." I deeply appreciated the intention behind this search, but it made me think that a far better question was, "How can my infant teach me to be mindful?" Your baby lives fully in the present moment—she stares intently at the faces around her, immediately reacts to noises and other stimuli, and (as best we know) is pretty much only concerned with her immediate needs.

Pay attention to how your baby pays attention to the world. What does she stare at? Can you imagine how your baby is taking in the landscape around her? Look deeply at the things that fascinate her, such as bright toys, ceiling fans, or pictures of faces, and see if you can find something fascinating about these common sights.

What noises interest her and/or soothe her? What noises startle her? What effect do those sounds have on you?

Let your baby help you see how truly fascinating our world is!

your baby lives fully in the present moment

closing words

We often say that mindfulness is simple, but not easy. Before even picking up this book, you likely understood the importance of being present, paying attention, responding wisely to difficulties, being kind to yourself, and not letting your thoughts and judgments get the better of you. But if all those things were easy, well, we wouldn't need all these books and instructions about how to do them!

Mindfulness is simple, but not easy. And because it's not easy, it's something we practice.

Each day, you can practice being present with your baby, perhaps simply by noticing how it feels to have his tiny hand in yours.

Each day, you can practice paying attention to your breath, your thoughts, your bodily sensations, and your emotions.

Each day, you can practice responding wisely in a difficult moment; if you're able to meet even one moment of challenge with a bit more presence and grace than the day before, it is a gift to yourself and everyone around you.

Each day, you can practice being kind to yourself, offering yourself forgiveness instead of judgment and criticism.

Each day, you can pause and notice thinking as thinking, judging as judging, and worrying as worrying.

It's in these simple practices that profound transformations can occur. I hope you are able to make the time and space for your mindfulness practice, so that you may experience these moments of greater calm, joy, and ease during this incredible time in your life.

As you embark on this journey of mindfulness and motherhood, I wish you and your baby all the best.

resources

Websites

Left Brain Buddha: The Modern Mindful Life

www.leftbrainbuddha.com

Author's blog.

Dr Dan Siegel

www.drdansiegel.com

Resources on mindfulness.

Greater Good Magazine: Science-based Insights for a Meaningful Life

greatergood.berkeley.edu

Articles on a range of topics, including mindfulness.

Mindful Magazine: Healthy Mind, Healthy Life

www.mindful.org

Articles on mindfulness in all areas of life.

Be Mindful

www.bemindful.co.uk

Search for courses on mindfulness near you in the UK.

Centre for Mindfulness Practice and Research UK

www.bangor.ac.uk/mindfulness

Updates on the latest research, including mindful parenting.

Apps

All the apps listed below are available for iOS and Android.

- **Headspace**
- **Ten Percent Happier**
- **Insight Timer**
- **Calm**

picture credits

pp. 1, 4 above, 16, 19, 20, 27, 48, 49, 59, 62, 75 below, 78, 97 © NotionPic/Shutterstock.com

pp. 2, 3, 4 below, 5 above, 6–7, 10–1, 40–1, 45, 56, 66–7, 69, 82–3, 90, 102–3, 104, 105, 106, 111, 112, 124–5 © Tanya Antusenok/Shutterstock.com

p. 79 © yellowline/Tanya Antusenok/Shutterstock.com

pp. 5 below, 88, 89, 117 © Naumova Marina/Shutterstock.com

pp. 8, 96 © Sasha Al/Shutterstock.com

pp. 13, 35, 37 © molotoka/Shutterstock.com

pp. 21, 50, 51, 61, 72, 74 © vectorstudi/Shutterstock.com

pp. 23, 36, 85, 98 © Ken Tackett/Shutterstock.com

pp. 22, 44 Illustration by Daniel Haskett © CICO Books

pp. 24, 25 © Pepe Gallardo/Shutterstock.com

p. 26 © Seahorse Vector/Shutterstock.com

p. 38 © Svetlana Kharchuk/Shutterstock.com

pp. 42, 68 © Biscotto Design/Shutterstock.com

p. 52 © Fagreia/Shutterstock.com

pp. 55, 71 © Mozaic Studio/Shutterstock.com

p. 60 © hoangpts/Shutterstock.com

p. 64 © Mariia Alexxandrova/Shutterstock.com

p. 75 above © Leria Kaleria/Shutterstock.com

pp. 76–77, 144 © CICO Books

p. 80 © MicroOne/Shutterstock.com

p. 81 © GoodStudio/Shutterstock.com

p. 92 © NADEZHDA VENEV/Shutterstock.com

p. 93 © WarmWorld/Shutterstock.com

p. 100 © Lytvynenko Anna/Shutterstock.com

p. 101 © Trendsetter Images/Shutterstock.com

p. 108 © Shutterstock.com

pp. 109, 127 © mentalmind/Shutterstock.com

p. 113 © Dmitry Lobanov/Shutterstock.com

p. 115 © bsd/Shutterstock.com

p. 119 © Evgeny Bornyakov/Shutterstock.com

p. 120 © Glinskaja Olga/Shutterstock.com

p. 121 © cosmaa/Shutterstock.com

index

acknowledgments

Thank you to the team at CICO for their work in seeing this book from conception to delivery. Thanks especially to Kristine Pidkameny, Carmel Edmonds, and Cindy Richards for your support, feedback, and commitment.

I came to the practice of mindfulness during my first pregnancy, in a small prenatal yoga studio in South Minneapolis. I will always be grateful for my first teachers who taught me how to simply be, during a time when I was so focused on all that I needed to do. Their words, patience, and wisdom completely changed my life. I have been lucky to continue to meet and learn from amazing mindfulness teachers, especially my colleagues at Mindful Schools. Alan Brown, Argos Gonzalez, Megan Sweet, and Erin Woo, you inspire me every day to be a better teacher and a better person. Thank you.

Finally, I am incredibly grateful to my family. As a writer, you'd think words would come easily, but in expressing just how much you all mean to me, I'm at a loss, so let me just say this: Todd, Abby, and Liam, you're simply the best.